Franklin Park School Library
District

In 1943 Louis Untermeyer made a selection from the work of Robert Frost, and added a biographical introduction as well as a running commentary on the poetry. This book, entitled *Come In,* was published by Henry Holt and Company. The New York *Sun* summarized it by saying, "The talents of a profound poet and a critic have gone to make a book which should hold a place beside the easy chairs of innumerable readers." Now Mr. Untermeyer has extended *Come In* especially for Washington Square Press, Inc., and the present volume contains thirty additional poems and a greatly enlarged commentary.

ILLUSTRATED BY JOHN O'HARA COSGRAVE II

Robert Frost has recently recorded many of his most popular poems. His years of successful platform reading show in his natural but subtle rendering of his seemingly simple verses. Detailed information concerning these records, which are available on both long-playing 33⅓ rpm and standard 78 rpm discs, can be obtained by writing to:

The National Council of Teachers
of English
508 South Sixth Street
Champaign, Illinois

A POCKET BOOK OF

Robert Frost's
POEMS

With an Introduction and Commentary by
LOUIS UNTERMEYER

WASHINGTON SQUARE PRESS, INC. • NEW YORK

A Pocket Book of Robert Frost's Poems

1960

5th printing......................January, 1963

A new edition of a distinguished literary work now made available in an inexpensive, well-designed format

The poems quoted in this volume are from *A Boy's Will, North of Boston, Mountain Interval, New Hampshire, West-running Brook, A Further Range, A Witness Tree, Come In, Steeple Bush,* and *In the Clearing.* No part of this book may be reproduced in any form without permission from the original publisher, Holt, Rinehart & Winston, Inc.

L

Published by

Washington Square Press, Inc.: Executive Offices, 630 Fifth Avenue
University Press Division, 32 Washington Place, New York, N.Y.

WASHINGTON SQUARE PRESS editions are distributed in the U.S. by Affiliated Publishers, a division of Pocket Books, Inc., 630 Fifth Avenue, New York 20, N.Y.

Copyright, 1930, 1939, 1943, 1946, 1949, by Henry Holt and Company, Inc. Copyright, 1936, 1949, ©, 1955, 1956, 1959, 1960, 1961, 1962, by Robert Frost. This WASHINGTON SQUARE PRESS *edition is published by arrangement with Holt, Rinehart & Winston, Inc. Printed in the U.S.A.*

CONTENTS

IV. STOPPING BY WOODS AND OTHER PLACES

A POCKET BOOK OF

Robert Frost's
POEMS

I

AN INTRODUCTION

ROBERT FROST: THE MAN AND THE POET

The character, as well as the career, of Robert Frost gives the lie to the usual misconceptions of the poet. Frost has been no less the ordinary man for being an extraordinary creator.

The creator, the artist, the extraordinary man, is merely the ordinary man intensified: a person whose life is sometimes lifted to a high pitch of feeling and who has the gift of making others share his excitement. The ordinary man lives by the creative spirit. He thinks in images and dreams in fantasy; he lives by poetry. Yet he seems to distrust it. He clings to the notion that a poet is a queer and incompetent creature, a daydreaming ne'er-do-well, an eccentric trying to escape the business of the everyday world, a soft and coddled soul.

Almost the opposite is true. History is the record of men who were not only poets but workers, men of action, discoverers, dreamers and doers. Sir Walter Raleigh's exploration of Guiana and other expeditions in the New World brought him fame and envy. Sir Philip Sidney was a soldier whose gallantry on the field of battle is a deathless story. Geoffrey Chaucer, "father of English poetry," was a diplomat and secret agent on the king's business in Europe. John Milton was Cromwell's fighting foreign secretary.

Nor have poets failed in labor and industry. Ben Jonson was a bricklayer. Robert Herrick was a jeweler. Robert Burns was a plowboy. William Blake designed, printed, and sold his own books. William Morris manufactured furniture.

Long before he became known as the greatest American poet of his time, Robert Frost worked as a farmer, a bobbin boy in a Massachusetts mill, a shoemaker, and a teacher in country schools.

Any account of Robert Frost's life must begin with its curious contradictions. Descended from a long line of New Englanders who were rooted in the region since 1632, Frost was born in California. The most American of poets, he was first recognized not in his own country, but abroad, and his first two books were published in England. He has never entered a competition and does not believe in prize contests, yet the Pulitzer Prize for the best poetry of the year has been awarded to him four times. His blank verse monologues are supposed to be written in "the rough, conversational tones of speech," yet his lyrics are remarkable for their delicate and precise music. He has chosen one part of the country for his special province—the very titles of his books seem local: *North of Boston, Mountain Interval, New Hampshire, A Further Range*—yet no poetry so regional has ever been so universal.

Robert Frost's ancestors were Scotch-English. His mother was of a Scottish seafaring family of Orkneyan origin, a schoolteacher whose name appears in most records as Isabelle Moody. Frost was more than fifty when he learned the correct spelling from a distant cousin in New Zealand; the relation from down under informed him that the proper spelling was "Moodie." A few years later the poet acknowledged the correction in a poem which serves as "motto" for *A Witness Tree*, a poem playfully signed "The Moodie Forester."

A restless and sometimes rebellious spirit possessed Frost's father. The family hoped that William Prescott Frost would be a lawyer, but he became a teacher, then an editor, then a politician. Revolting from Republican New England, Frost's father went to the west coast and worked on the San Francisco *Bulletin,* a Democratic newspaper. During the Civil War, he was proud to be a Copperhead, a southern sympathizer and champion of states' rights. When his son was born on March 26, 1874, the child was named after the great southern soldier and scholar, and christened Robert Lee Frost.

The San Francisco of Frost's youth was a rough town—Westerners sported revolvers as jauntily as Easterners carried canes—and, although Frost's father enjoyed the hazardous life of editor-politician in a boisterous community, his health did not stand the strain. When he died of tuberculosis in his early thirties, the boy Robert was ten years old.

ii

Taken back by his mother to the New England of his ancestors, the fatherless boy grew into the independent young man. His mother taught school and read to him. The first story he ever read through for himself was *Scottish Chiefs;* the second was *Tom Brown's School Days.* He was then fourteen, a late starter with books. He discovered poetry, and relished the sheer music of Poe as much as the meaningfulness of Emerson. Simultaneously with the discovery, he began to write his own verse. At fifteen he saw his first poem printed in the Lawrence *High School Bulletin;* it was a long ballad about the night when Cortez was driven out of Mexico City. When he was nineteen his first "professional" poem was accepted by *The Independent,* a magazine of national circulation; he received a check for fifteen dollars. His mother was proud, but the rest of the

4

family were alarmed. His grandfather said, "No one can make a living at poetry. But I tell you what," he added shrewdly, "we'll give you a year to make a go of it. And you'll have to promise to quit writing if you can't make a success of it in a year. What do you say?"

"Give me twenty—give me twenty," replied the nineteen-year-old youth, like an auctioneer.

Someone must have overheard the mocking flippancy and punished him by making him wait the full twenty years. Twenty years later, almost to the month, Robert Frost's first book, *A Boy's Will*, was published and proved that the boy was not only a true poet but an accurate prophet.

Meanwhile he grew up among his fellows. He graduated at seventeen from the Lawrence High School, and delivered the valedictory. His covaledictorian was a remarkably pretty girl, Elinor Miriam White. Three years later he married her.

His had been a crowded youth. In school vacation days, from twelve on, he had worked in the shoe shops of Salem, New Hampshire, nailing shanks and cutting heels, helping on the farm with the haying, and pushing a bobbin wagon in a woolen mill in Lawrence, Massachusetts. But, long before he was eighteen, Frost knew what he wanted to do; he literally attached himself to poetry. First he made an attempt to please the family, especially his father's father, and get a formal education. After being graduated from high school, he entered Dartmouth College. Within two months he was back home. "I was mostly roughing around up there," he said years later. "My mother had a hard school to teach. She had a lot of rough boys, and teaching them was the least part of her work. I told myself—perhaps as an excuse—that if I had to be roughing some place, I'd be more useful roughing around that school than roughing around at college." So, at eighteen, Robert Frost came back and took his mother's class away from her in the school at Methuen, Massachusetts.

Although his father's father was willing to help him, Robert was not willing to take the advice that went with the help. He might be told what to do, but never how to do it. Instead, he contributed to the family income by teaching at one school and another, by working in Lawrence, reporting for the town newspaper, editing a "column" of notes and sketches. One of his stories concerned a large bird in a big wind that, looking for a perch, flew to the top of the flagpole of a large building and stayed there until some hunting fool shot him. The building was the U. S. Post Office, the flag was flying, and the bird was an American eagle.

iii

Two years after his marriage, Robert Frost once more tried to please the family and complete his scholastic education. He entered Harvard in his twenty-second year and remained until his twenty-fourth. He liked the study of philosophy; he was drawn to the classics; he enjoyed Latin and Greek. But—"It wasn't what I wanted," he said.

His grandfather was disappointed, but he gave his unambitious grandson a farm near Derry, New Hampshire, for a refuge. The refuge presented something of a challenge, and at twenty-five Frost began farming. He was anything but a born tiller of the soil, though he did make some sort of living exclusively as a farmer for five or six years. In the end he turned to teaching part of the time. But his head was full of poems, and his wife was only too willing he should write. Everyone was displeased—except himself and his wife, neither of whom minded being "neglected."

IN NEGLECT

They leave us so to the way we took,
  As two in whom they were proved mistaken,
That we sit sometimes in the wayside nook,
With mischievous, vagrant, seraphic look,
  And *try* if we cannot feel forsaken.

iv

The Derry farm had been given Frost on such terms that
he was committed to it for ten years. Ten years passed and
Frost, now thirty-five, was able to sell his New Hampshire
property. With the money, plus the little he had saved by
teaching at Pinkerton Academy in Derry Village, Frost
uprooted himself and his family, and sailed for England.
Living abroad was cheap—this was in 1912—and Mrs. Frost
wanted, she said, "to live under thatch." The Frosts found
a home in Beaconsfield, a little town in rural Buckingham-
shire. Although England was in the throes of a literary
revival and "Georgian Poetry" was the center of a move-
ment, the Frosts were untouched by what was going on.
They went nowhere, except for occasional visits to London,
and saw no one until almost a year had passed. Then they
tried farming again, this time in Gloucestershire, where
their near neighbors were the poet-dramatist Lascelles
Abercrombie and the poet Wilfrid Wilson Gibson.
  One evening in 1913 Frost sat before an open fire, shuf-
fling through the poems he had written, only a few of which

had been printed in magazines. In his hands was the work of twenty years. "It came to me that maybe someone would publish a few of these poems in a book. It really hadn't ever occurred to me before that this might be done." Frost remembered that Henley's publisher had been David Nutt. David Nutt was dead, but his widow was carrying on the publishing business, and to Mrs. Nutt he went. Mrs. Nutt read the work of the unknown poet and decided to publish his book.

It was as simple as that. Too simple, perhaps—no influential friends; no publicity; nothing to win favor except the poetry. But young authors impatient for publication should remember that Frost had to wait more than twenty years from the time of his first poem in a high school magazine to the time of his first book. When the volume appeared, the poet was thirty-eight years old.

v

A Boy's Will is Robert Frost's first book, and the title not only indicates the mood but pays a tribute to Longfellow who, in "My Lost Youth," wrote:

> A boy's will is the wind's will,
> And the thoughts of youth are long, long thoughts.

The English reviewers were captivated with Frost's unaffected lyrics, with his simple vocabulary and sharp observation, most of all with his way of turning usually forgotten thoughts into unforgettable phrases. But if the critics were enthusiastic about *A Boy's Will*, they were exuberant about

8

North of Boston, which appeared about a year later. They praised the second volume for many reasons. Wilfrid Wilson Gibson wrote, "Mr. Frost has turned the living speech of men and women into poetry . . . Tales that might be mere anecdotes in the hands of another poet take on universal significance because of their native veracity and truth to local character." An anonymous critic in *The Nation* acclaimed the poems for their "downright knowledge, their vivid observation, and (most important) their rich enjoyment of all kinds of *practical* life." Attention was also directed to the plain language and lack of rhetoric, "the careful rendering into the meter of customary speech."

The last feature is Frost's most characteristic, if not his most enduring, quality. *A Boy's Will* is poetry that sings; *North of Boston* is poetry that talks. This was emphasized in an essay entitled "The Permanence of Robert Frost," by Mark Van Doren, who maintained that Frost's singularity, his "strangeness," consisted in the conversational tone he builds into his verse. "Whether in dialogue or in lyric, his poems are people talking. . . . The man who talks under the name of Robert Frost knows how to say a great deal in a short space, just as the many men and women whom he has listened to in New England and elsewhere have known how to express in the few words they use more truth than volumes of ordinary rhetoric can express."

vi

In early 1915, seven months after the outbreak of the First World War, Robert Frost returned to America. He came back to find himself suddenly and unexpectedly famous. His two books were on sale everywhere in the United States, published by a New York publisher, Henry Holt and Company. The man who had left America an unknown writer came back to be hailed a leader of "the new era in American poetry."

As soon as Frost suspected he might now live by poetry alone, he did a characteristic thing: he bought a farm. It was on a hillside near Franconia, in the White Mountains of New Hampshire. He lived there for five years.

Less than a year after his return from England, Frost delivered the Phi Beta Kappa poem at Tufts College. The year following he was invited to join the advisory board of the short-lived but brilliant monthly, *The Seven Arts;* he was elected to the National Institute of Arts and Letters; he was the Phi Beta Kappa poet at Harvard, the very college from which he had declined to graduate. "Truly," wrote Gorham B. Munson in 1927, "he had scarcely tapped, and all the doors of literary America opened to him."

Frost was now forty. During the next twenty years—from 1916 to 1936—the poet spent much of his time at various institutions of learning. Although nominally engaged as a professor, he was a stimulator rather than a teacher. His function was not to instruct but to excite, to infuse with warmth, to act as "a sort of poetic radiator." This function he richly fulfilled. Without ceasing to create, he became a critical force; never trying to persuade anyone, he became an influence.

In 1938 he moved to Boston, Massachusetts, and three years later took a house in Cambridge. But he did not relinquish his hold upon the land. He now owned, and occasionally occupied, five farms—all in Vermont.

The volumes that followed *North of Boston* marked a continual increase in the ability to make verse talk and sing. Sometimes the poems conversed; sometimes they made their own tunes; mostly they talked and sang together.

Poets are said to lose the singing impulse as they grow older. The reverse is true with Frost; his later work is distinguished by its lyrical power. *A Witness Tree,* published in Frost's sixty-seventh year, is as fresh as anything written in his youth.

Four times Frost was awarded the Pulitzer Prize for the best book of poetry of the year—Frost being the only poet ever to achieve that quadruple distinction—in 1924, for *New Hampshire;* in 1931, for *Collected Poems;* in 1937, for *A Further Range;* and in 1943, for *A Witness Tree.* Other honors steadily accumulated. He was intermittently on the faculty at Amherst College from 1916 to 1938; Poet in Residence at Michigan University from 1921 to 1923 and again during 1925-26; he delivered the Charles Eliot Norton lectures at Harvard in 1936. He was cofounder of the now famous Bread Loaf School of English—a summer institution in the Green Mountains of Vermont—and he has lectured there since 1920. He was awarded honorary degrees by Columbia, Dartmouth, Yale, Harvard, and other colleges and universities. He was one of the few authors to receive the Gold Medal from the National Institute of Arts and Letters.

These honors did not affect the man or his work. The quiet strength, the deep convictions, remained unshaken in the person as well as in the poetry. The last lines of the first poem in Frost's first book took on a prophetic conclusiveness:

They would not find me changed from him they knew—
Only more sure of all I thought was true.

The truth has been Frost's central passion. He has never been fooled by easy solutions or tricked by slogans; he has never given in to the fashion of the moment in poetry or politics. Again and again he has reaffirmed his belief; he states part of it in "The Black Cottage":

> . . . why abandon a belief
> Merely because it ceases to be true.
> Cling to it long enough, and not a doubt
> It will turn true again, for so it goes.
> Most of the change we think we see in life
> Is due to truths being in and out of favor.
> As I sit here, and oftentimes, I wish
> I could be monarch of a desert land
> I could devote and dedicate forever
> To the truths we keep coming back and back to.

But a persistent search for truths does not mean that Frost is a grim philosopher. On the contrary, his touch is as light as it is certain. It is light even when—or especially when— his subject is tragic. When Frost is most serious, he is most casual. His verse has a growing intimacy; it radiates an honest neighborliness in which wit and wisdom are joined. He

12

knows humanity without its "company manners"; he has studied it in stony pastures and academies of art and science. He appreciates skill in every craft. Preferring reality of experience to a retreat to a fantastic dream-world, he insists:

The fact is the sweetest dream that labor knows.

Always the worker as well as the dreamer, Frost shapes his verse and judges a poem by the same standards which, says T. K. Whipple, "he would apply to an ax or a hoe or a spade: it must be solid, strong, honest." The pulse of his verse is timed to the heartbeat of the workaday world. Poetry and action, love and need, are united. As the poet himself says at the end of "Two Tramps in Mud Time":

> But yield who will to their separation,
> My object in living is to unite
> My avocation and my vocation
> As my two eyes make one in sight.
> Only where love and need are one,
> And the work is play for mortal stakes,
> Is the deed ever really done
> For Heaven and the future's sakes.

Frost judges, but he rarely condemns; he is fundamentally serious, but never pompous. Some critics have considered him essentially a moralist, but his worst enemy (if he has one) would not accuse him of trying to make anything or anyone over. He accepts the world's contradictions without being crushed by them. One of his most recent poems, significantly entitled "The Lesson for Today," is a long philosophical discussion, which concludes:

And were an epitaph to be my story
I'd have a short one ready for my own.
I would have written of me on my stone:
I had a lover's quarrel with the world.

"I had a lover's quarrel with the world." No reviewer has written, none will write, a more accurate summary of the poet's spirit; a contemplation of the world which is free to question, even to criticize, but always with understanding, always with earnest love.

—Louis Untermeyer

AN INVITATION

THE PASTURE

I'm going out to clean the pasture spring;
I'll only stop to rake the leaves away
(And wait to watch the water clear, I may):
I sha'n't be gone long.—You come too.

I'm going out to fetch the little calf
That's standing by the mother. It's so young,
It totters when she licks it with her tongue.
I sha'n't be gone long.—You come too.

II

THE CODE AND OTHER STORIES

Robert Frost has written on almost every subject. He has illuminated things as common as a woodpile and as uncommon as a prehistoric pebble, as natural as a bird singing in its sleep and as "mechanistic" as the revolt of a factory worker. But his central subject is humanity. His poetry lives with a particular aliveness because it expresses living people. Other poets have written *about* people. But Robert Frost's poems *are* the people; they work, and walk about, and converse, and tell their stories with the freedom of common speech.

This is a poetry that never pretends. It is the poetry of good conversation; it is a language of things as well as thoughts. Frost the speaker is well described by another poet, Wilfrid Wilson Gibson, who, in "The Golden Room," pictures a meeting of the American and a few of his English poet-friends:

>   . . . In the lamplight
> We talked and laughed, but for the most part listened
> While Robert Frost kept on and on and on
> In his slow New England fashion for our delight,
> Holding us with shrewd turns and racy quips,
> And the rare twinkle of his grave blue eyes.
>
> We sat there in the lamplight while the day
> Died from rose-latticed casements, and the plovers
> Called over the low meadows till the owls
> Answered them from the elms; we sat and talked—
> Now a quick flash from Abercrombie, now
> A murmured dry half-heard aside from Thomas,
> Now a clear laughing word from Brooke, and then
> Again Frost's rich and ripe philosophy
> That had the body and tang of good draught-cider
> And poured as clear a stream.

This "rich and ripe philosophy," this sense of universal understanding, is in everything Frost has written, even the earliest. "The Tuft of Flowers," a poem in his first volume, expresses the whole spirit of human participation. Even those who think they work alone, apart from others, have more than they know in common.

> "Men work together," I told him from the heart,
> "Whether they work together or apart."

Here, in the flight of a butterfly and the whispering of an unseen scythe, is the fulfillment of kinship, a human questioning and the brotherly reply.

THE TUFT OF FLOWERS

I went to turn the grass once after one
Who mowed it in the dew before the sun.

The dew was gone that made his blade so keen
Before I came to view the levelled scene.

I looked for him behind an isle of trees;
I listened for his whetstone on the breeze.

But he had gone his way, the grass all mown,
And I must be, as he had been,—alone,

"As all must be," I said within my heart,
"Whether they work together or apart."

But as I said it, swift there passed me by
On noiseless wing a bewildered butterfly,

Seeking with memories grown dim o'er night
Some resting flower of yesterday's delight.

And once I marked his flight go round and round,
As where some flower lay withering on the ground.

And then he flew as far as eye could see,
And then on tremulous wing came back to me.

I thought of questions that have no reply,
And would have turned to toss the grass to dry;

But he turned first, and led my eye to look
At a tall tuft of flowers beside a brook,

A leaping tongue of bloom the scythe had spared
Beside a reedy brook the scythe had bared.

I left my place to know them by their name,
Finding them butterfly weed when I came.

The mower in the dew had loved them thus,
Leaving them to flourish, not for us,

Nor yet to draw one thought of ours to him,
But from sheer morning gladness at the brim.

The butterfly and I had lit upon,
Nevertheless, a message from the dawn,

That made me hear the wakening birds around,
And hear his long scythe whispering to the ground,

And feel a spirit kindred to my own;
So that henceforth I worked no more alone;

But glad with him, I worked as with his aid,
And weary, sought at noon with him the shade;

And dreaming, as it were, held brotherly speech
With one whose thought I had not hoped to reach.

"Men work together," I told him from the heart,
"Whether they work together or apart."

"Blueberries" is an odd sort of narrative, a story of a family told entirely in dialogue. The Lorens are seen through the eyes of two neighbors who are a little vexed and more than a little amused at the thrifty tricks of father Loren and his seemingly innocent tribe.

Although the poem does not attempt to teach anything, the city-bred reader will learn several things he may have missed knowing. He will discover how the berrypicker gets his berries. He will realize that a "democrat-load" is not a political comment, but a light wagon with two removable seats and too cheap to afford a top. He will be led to find out that the chewink is a kind of finch and is so called because of its note, which is accented on the second syllable. And why (unless for the rhyme) does the poet refer to the chewink rather than to any other kind of bird? Because the poet is "versed in country things" and knows that the chewink has a quick eye and an appetite for berries, especially blueberries.

BLUEBERRIES

"You ought to have seen what I saw on my way
To the village, through Patterson's pasture to-day:
Blueberries as big as the end of your thumb,
Real sky-blue, and heavy, and ready to drum
In the cavernous pail of the first one to come!
And all ripe together, not some of them green
And some of them ripe! You ought to have seen!"

"I don't know what part of the pasture you mean."

"You know where they cut off the woods—let me see—
It was two years ago—or no!—can it be
No longer than that?—and the following fall
The fire ran and burned it all up but the wall."

"Why, there hasn't been time for the bushes to grow.
That's always the way with the blueberries, though:
There may not have been the ghost of a sign
Of them anywhere under the shade of the pine,
But get the pine out of the way, you may burn
The pasture all over until not a fern
Or grass-blade is left, not to mention a stick,
And presto, they're up all around you as thick
And hard to explain as a conjuror's trick."

"It must be on charcoal they fatten their fruit.
I taste in them sometimes the flavour of soot.
And after all really they're ebony skinned:
The blue's but a mist from the breath of the wind,
A tarnish that goes at a touch of the hand,
And less than the tan with which pickers are tanned."

"Does Patterson know what he has, do you think?"

"He may and not care and so leave the chewink
To gather them for him—you know what he is.
He won't make the fact that they're rightfully his
An excuse for keeping us other folk out."

"I wonder you didn't see Loren about."

"The best of it was that I did. Do you know,
I was just getting through what the field had to show
And over the wall and into the road,
When who should come by, with a democrat-load
Of all the young chattering Lorens alive,
But Loren, the fatherly, out for a drive."

"He saw you, then? What did he do? Did he frown?"

"He just kept nodding his head up and down.
You know how politely he always goes by.
But he thought a big thought—I could tell by his eye—
Which being expressed, might be this in effect:
'I have left those there berries, I shrewdly suspect,
To ripen too long. I am greatly to blame.'"

"He's a thriftier person than some I could name."

"He seems to be thrifty; and hasn't he need,
With the mouths of all those young Lorens to feed?
He has brought them all up on wild berries, they say,
Like birds. They store a great many away.
They eat them the year round, and those they don't eat
They sell in the store and buy shoes for their feet."

"Who cares what they say? It's a nice way to live,
Just taking what Nature is willing to give,
Not forcing her hand with harrow and plow."

"I wish you had seen his perpetual bow—
And the air of the youngsters! Not one of them turned,
And they looked so solemn-absurdly concerned."

"I wish I knew half what the flock of them know
Of where all the berries and other things grow,
Cranberries in bogs and raspberries on top
Of the boulder-strewn mountain, and when they will crop.
I met them one day and each had a flower
Stuck into his berries as fresh as a shower;
Some strange kind—they told me it hadn't a name."

"I've told you how once not long after we came,
I almost provoked poor Loren to mirth
By going to him of all people on earth
To ask if he knew any fruit to be had
For the picking. The rascal, he said he'd be glad
To tell if he knew. But the year had been bad.
There *had* been some berries—but those were all gone.
He didn't say where they had been. He went on:
'I'm sure—I'm sure'—as polite as could be.
He spoke to his wife in the door, 'Let me see,
Mame, *we* don't know any good berrying place?'
It was all he could do to keep a straight face."

"If he thinks all the fruit that grows wild is for him,
He'll find he's mistaken. See here, for a whim,
We'll pick in the Pattersons' pasture this year.
We'll go in the morning, that is, if it's clear,

And the sun shines out warm: the vines must be wet.
It's so long since I picked I almost forget
How we used to pick berries: we took one look round,
Then sank out of sight like trolls underground,
And saw nothing more of each other, or heard,
Unless when you said I was keeping a bird
Away from its nest, and I said it was you.
'Well, one of us is.' For complaining it flew
Around and around us. And then for a while
We picked, till I feared you had wandered a mile,
And I thought I had lost you. I lifted a shout
Too loud for the distance you were, it turned out,
For when you made answer, your voice was as low
As talking—you stood up beside me, you know."

"We sha'n't have the place to ourselves to enjoy—
Not likely, when all the young Lorens deploy.
They'll be there to-morrow, or even to-night.
They won't be too friendly—they may be polite—
To people they look on as having no right
To pick where they're picking. But we won't complain.
You ought to have seen how it looked in the rain,
The fruit mixed with water in layers of leaves,
Like two kinds of jewels, a vision for thieves."

A good poem delights us in many ways and for many reasons. It may arrest us by startling; it may win our affection by comforting; it may hold us by telling a true story or persuading us about something too good—or too wild—to be true. But it is the way of telling that makes one poet differ from another, and makes poetry differ from verse. It is the combination of the strange and the familiar that is the chief power of poetry: the power of surprise.

In "Home Burial" the strange and the familiar are strikingly blended. The talk is the talk of everyday, the accents of a man and wife facing some sort of crisis; but the situation is strange—common in words, uncommon in experience. Little details take on unusual meanings: the sight of the graveyard "so small the window frames the whole of it"; the quickly piled burial mound with the gravel "leaping" in the air. Even the stains of mud on the man's shoes take on a significance that, to the woman, is horrifying because it is so matter-of-fact.

He saw her from the bottom of the stairs
Before she saw him. She was starting down,
Looking back over her shoulder at some fear.
She took a doubtful step and then undid it
To raise herself and look again. He spoke
Advancing toward her: "What is it you see
From up there always—for I want to know."
She turned and sank upon her skirts at that,
And her face changed from terrified to dull.
He said to gain time: "What is it you see,"
Mounting until she cowered under him.
"I will find out now—you must tell me, dear."
She, in her place, refused him any help
With the least stiffening of her neck and silence
She let him look, sure that he wouldn't see,
Blind creature; and a while he didn't see.
But at last he murmured, "Oh," and again, "Oh."

"What is it—what?" she said.

                              "Just that I see."

"You don't," she challenged. "Tell me what it is."

"The wonder is I didn't see at once.
I never noticed it from here before.
I must be wonted to it—that's the reason.
The little graveyard where my people are!
So small the window frames the whole of it.

Not so much larger than a bedroom, is it?
There are three stones of slate and one of marble,
Broad-shouldered little slabs there in the sunlight
On the sidehill. We haven't to mind *those*.
But I understand: it is not the stones,
But the child's mound—"

"Don't, don't, don't, don't," she cried.

She withdrew shrinking from beneath his arm
That rested on the banister, and slid downstairs;
And turned on him with such a daunting look,
He said twice over before he knew himself:
"Can't a man speak of his own child he's lost?"

"Not you! Oh, where's my hat? Oh, I don't need it!
I must get out of here. I must get air.
I don't know rightly whether any man can."

"Amy! Don't go to someone else this time.
Listen to me. I won't come down the stairs."
He sat and fixed his chin between his fists.
"There's something I should like to ask you, dear."

"You don't know how to ask it."

"Help me, then."

Her fingers moved the latch for all reply.

"My words are nearly always an offence.
I don't know how to speak of anything

So as to please you. But I might be taught
I should suppose. I can't say I see how.
A man must partly give up being a man
With women-folk. We could have some arrangement
By which I'd bind myself to keep hands off
Anything special you're a-mind to name.
Though I don't like such things 'twixt those that love.
Two that don't love can't live together without them.
But two that do can't live together with them."
She moved the latch a little. "Don't—don't go.
Don't carry it to someone else this time.
Tell me about it if it's something human.
Let me into your grief. I'm not so much
Unlike other folks as your standing there
Apart would make me out. Give me my chance.
I do think, though, you overdo it a little.
What was it brought you up to think it the thing
To take your mother-loss of a first child
So inconsolably—in the face of love.
You'd think his memory might be satisfied—"

"There you go sneering now!"

                              "I'm not, I'm not!
You make me angry. I'll come down to you.
God, what a woman! And it's come to this,
A man can't speak of his own child that's dead."

"You can't because you don't know how to speak.
If you had any feelings, you that dug
With your own hand—how could you?—his little grave;
I saw you from that very window there,

28

Making the gravel leap and leap in air,
Leap up, like that, like that, and land so lightly
And roll back down the mound beside the hole.
I thought, Who is that man? I didn't know you.
And I crept down the stairs and up the stairs
To look again, and still your spade kept lifting.
Then you came in. I heard your rumbling voice
Out in the kitchen, and I don't know why,
But I went near to see with my own eyes.
You could sit there with the stains on your shoes
Of the fresh earth from your own baby's grave
And talk about your everyday concerns.
You had stood the spade up against the wall
Outside there in the entry, for I saw it."

"I shall laugh the worst laugh I ever laughed.
I'm cursed. God, if I don't believe I'm cursed."

"I can repeat the very words you were saying.
'Three foggy mornings and one rainy day
Will rot the best birch fence a man can build.'
Think of it, talk like that at such a time!
What had how long it takes a birch to rot
To do with what was in the darkened parlour.
You *couldn't* care! The nearest friends can go
With anyone to death, comes so far short
They might as well not try to go at all.
No, from the time when one is sick to death,
One is alone, and he dies more alone.
Friends make pretence of following to the grave,
But before one is in it, their minds are turned
And making the best of their way back to life

29

And living people, and things they understand.
But the world's evil. I won't have grief so
If I can change it. Oh, I won't, I won't!"

"There, you have said it all and you feel better.
You won't go now. You're crying. Close the door.
The heart's gone out of it: why keep it up.
Amy! There's someone coming down the road!"

"*You*—oh, you think the talk is all. I must go—
Somewhere out of this house. How can I make you—"

"If—you—do!" She was opening the door wider.
"Where do you mean to go? First tell me that.
I'll follow and bring you back by force. I *will!*—"

Many attempts have been made to define Realism, and no two definitions have agreed with each other. It seems safe to say that a realist is one who really knows what he is talking about. If this is true, Frost is a realist, for no American writer knows his subjects, people and places, so thoroughly. But his is a peculiar kind of realism. It does not insist on a catalogue of mean trifles, on a piling up of bald or brutal details. "There are two types of realist," Frost once said. "There is the one who offers a good deal of dirt with his potato to show that it is a real potato. And there is the one who is satisfied with the potato brushed clean. I am inclined to be the second kind. To me, the thing that art does for life is to clean it, to strip it to form."

At another time he remarked, with a half-joking reference to the poetic terms in textbooks, "Instead of a Realist—if I must be classified—I think I might better be called a Synecdochist; for I am fond of the synecdoche in poetry, that figure of speech in which we use a part for the whole."

That playful statement might be a key to Frost's method: "a part for the whole." Without telling all, he *suggests* all. "All that an artist needs is samples."

Frost's stories are "samples." They are not novels in verse. They do not pretend to describe life from the cradle to the grave; they are pieces of life—"a part for the whole." Frost rarely insists or explains; he never says too much. Such stories as "The Witch of Coös" and "Paul's Wife" are told by holding back some of the facts. They are all the better as stories (and as art) because the narrator uses suggestion and understatement: he is not saying all he knows and he is not telling all he feels.

"The Witch of Coös" is one of the strangest of narratives, so incredible and yet so plausible. It is a ghost story, and its homeliness is its surprise. No other tone could be so effective, for it casually mixes prattle with terror.

THE WITCH OF COÖS

I staid the night for shelter at a farm
Behind the mountain, with a mother and son,
Two old-believers. They did all the talking.

MOTHER. Folks think a witch who has familiar spirits
She could call up to pass a winter evening,
But won't, should be burned at the stake or something.
Summoning spirits isn't "Button, button,
Who's got the button," I would have them know.

SON. Mother can make a common table rear
And kick with two legs like an army mule.

MOTHER. And when I've done it, what good have I done?
Rather than tip a table for you, let me
Tell you what Ralle the Sioux Control once told me.
He said the dead had souls, but when I asked him
How could that be—I thought the dead were souls,
He broke my trance. Don't that make you suspicious
That there's something the dead are keeping back?
Yes, there's something the dead are keeping back.

SON. You wouldn't want to tell him what we have
Up attic, mother?

MOTHER. Bones—a skeleton.

SON. But the headboard of mother's bed is pushed
Against the attic door: the door is nailed.

It's harmless. Mother hears it in the night
Halting perplexed behind the barrier
Of door and headboard. Where it wants to get
Is back into the cellar where it came from.

MOTHER. We'll never let them, will we, son! We'll never!

SON. It left the cellar forty years ago
And carried itself like a pile of dishes
Up one flight from the cellar to the kitchen,
Another from the kitchen to the bedroom,
Another from the bedroom to the attic,
Right past both father and mother, and neither stopped it.
Father had gone upstairs; mother was downstairs.
I was a baby: I don't know where I was.

MOTHER. The only fault my husband found with me—
I went to sleep before I went to bed,
Especially in winter when the bed
Might just as well be ice and the clothes snow.
The night the bones came up the cellar-stairs
Toffile had gone to bed alone and left me,
But left an open door to cool the room off
So as to sort of turn me out of it.
I was just coming to myself enough
To wonder where the cold was coming from,
When I heard Toffile upstairs in the bedroom
And thought I heard him downstairs in the cellar.
The board we had laid down to walk dry-shod on
When there was water in the cellar in spring
Struck the hard cellar bottom. And then someone
Began the stairs, two footsteps for each step,

The way a man with one leg and a crutch,
Or a little child, comes up. It wasn't Toffile:
It wasn't anyone who could be there.
The bulkhead double-doors were double-locked
And swollen tight and buried under snow.
The cellar windows were banked up with sawdust
And swollen tight and buried under snow.
It was the bones. I knew them—and good reason.
My first impulse was to get to the knob
And hold the door. But the bones didn't try
The door; they halted helpless on the landing,
Waiting for things to happen in their favor.
The faintest restless rustling ran all through them.
I never could have done the thing I did
If the wish hadn't been too strong in me
To see how they were mounted for this walk.
I had a vision of them put together
Not like a man, but like a chandelier.
So suddenly I flung the door wide on him.
A moment he stood balancing with emotion,
And all but lost himself. (A tongue of fire
Flashed out and licked along his upper teeth.
Smoke rolled inside the sockets of his eyes.)
Then he came at me with one hand outstretched,
The way he did in life once; but this time
I struck the hand off brittle on the floor,
And fell back from him on the floor myself.
The finger-pieces slid in all directions.
(Where did I see one of those pieces lately?
Hand me my button-box—it must be there.)
I sat up on the floor and shouted, "Toffile,
It's coming up to you." It had its choice

Of the door to the cellar or the hall.
It took the hall door for the novelty,
And set off briskly for so slow a thing,
Still going every which way in the joints, though,
So that it looked like lightning or a scribble,
From the slap I had just now given its hand.
I listened till it almost climbed the stairs
From the hall to the only finished bedroom,
Before I got up to do anything;
Then ran and shouted, "Shut the bedroom door,
Toffile, for my sake!" "Company?" he said,
"Don't make me get up; I'm too warm in bed."
So lying forward weakly on the handrail
I pushed myself upstairs, and in the light
(The kitchen had been dark) I had to own
I could see nothing. "Toffile, I don't see it.
It's with us in the room though. It's the bones."
"What bones?" "The cellar bones—out of the grave."
That made him throw his bare legs out of bed
And sit up by me and take hold of me.
I wanted to put out the light and see
If I could see it, or else mow the room,
With our arms at the level of our knees,
And bring the chalk-pile down. "I'll tell you what—
It's looking for another door to try.
The uncommonly deep snow has made him think
Of his old song, *The Wild Colonial Boy*,
He always used to sing along the tote-road.
He's after an open door to get out-doors.
Let's trap him with an open door up attic."
Toffile agreed to that, and sure enough,
Almost the moment he was given an opening,

The steps began to climb the attic stairs.
I heard them. Toffile didn't seem to hear them.
"Quick!" I slammed to the door and held the knob.
"Toffile, get nails." I made him nail the door shut,
And push the headboard of the bed against it.
Then we asked was there anything
Up attic that we'd ever want again.
The attic was less to us than the cellar.
If the bones liked the attic, let them have it.
Let them stay in the attic. When they sometimes
Come down the stairs at night and stand perplexed
Behind the door and headboard of the bed,
Brushing their chalky skull with chalky fingers,
With sounds like the dry rattling of a shutter,
That's what I sit up in the dark to say—
To no one any more since Toffile died.
Let them stay in the attic since they went there.
I promised Toffile to be cruel to them
For helping them be cruel once to him.

son. We think they had a grave down in the cellar.

MOTHER. We know they had a grave down in the cellar.

son. We never could find out whose bones they were.

MOTHER. Yes, we could too, son. Tell the truth for once
They were a man's his father killed for me.
I mean a man he killed instead of me.
The least I could do was to help dig their grave.
We were about it one night in the cellar.
Son knows the story: but 'twas not for him

To tell the truth, suppose the time had come.
Son looks surprised to see me end a lie
We'd kept all these years between ourselves
So as to have it ready for outsiders.
But tonight I don't care enough to lie—
I don't remember why I ever cared.
Toffile, if he were here, I don't believe
Could tell you why he ever cared himself . . .

She hadn't found the finger-bone she wanted
Among the buttons poured out in her lap.
I verified the name next morning: Toffile.
The rural letter-box said Toffile Lajway.

"Paul's Wife," unlike most of Frost's poems about country characters, is related to folklore and, specifically, to the swaggering folklore of the American frontier. However, instead of being a retelling of a tall tale, it is a new one. "Paul's Wife" supplies a fresh figure and reveals an unknown side of Paul Bunyan, the mythical giant of the logging camps. Many books have been written about the hero's adventures and his unbelievable exploits. They have told how the rocking of this superlumberjack's cradle made such waves in the sea that they almost drowned the villages on the Maine coast; how his griddle was so big that, in order to grease it, ten men had to skate on it with chunks of bacon strapped to their soles; how his trees were so tall it took a whole week to see to the tops.

But Robert Frost makes the story his own. He presents a something about Paul Bunyan which cannot be found in the books, an imaginative something as fantastic as any of the legends, but far more tender and touching, and stubbornly proud.

PAUL'S WIFE

To drive Paul out of any lumber camp
All that was needed was to say to him,
"How is the wife, Paul?"—and he'd disappear.
Some said it was because he had no wife,
And hated to be twitted on the subject.
Others because he'd come within a day
Or so of having one, and then been jilted.
Others because he'd had one once, a good one,
Who'd run away with someone else and left him.
And others still because he had one now
He only had to be reminded of,—
He was all duty to her in a minute:
He had to run right off to look her up,
As if to say, "That's so, how is my wife?
I hope she isn't getting into mischief."
No one was anxious to get rid of Paul.
He'd been the hero of the mountain camps
Ever since, just to show them, he had slipped
The bark of a whole tamarack off whole,
As clean as boys do off a willow twig
To make a willow whistle on a Sunday
In April by subsiding meadow brooks.
They seemed to ask him just to see him go,
"How is the wife, Paul?" and he always went.
He never stopped to murder anyone
Who asked the question. He just disappeared—
Nobody knew in what direction,
Although it wasn't usually long
Before they heard of him in some new camp,

The same Paul at the same old feats of logging.
The question everywhere was why should Paul
Object to being asked a civil question—
A man you could say almost anything to
Short of a fighting word. You have the answers.
And there was one more not so fair to Paul:
That Paul had married a wife not his equal.
Paul was ashamed of her. To match a hero,
She would have had to be a heroine;
Instead of which she was some half-breed squaw.
But if the story Murphy told was true,
She wasn't anything to be ashamed of.

You know Paul could do wonders. Everyone's
Heard how he thrashed the horses on a load
That wouldn't budge until they simply stretched
Their rawhide harness from the load to camp.
Paul told the boss the load would be all right,
"The sun will bring your load in"—and it did—
By shrinking the rawhide to natural length.
That's what is called a stretcher. But I guess
The one about his jumping so's to land
With both his feet at once against the ceiling,
And then land safely right side up again,
Back on the floor, is fact or pretty near fact.
Well this is such a yarn. Paul sawed his wife
Out of a white-pine log. Murphy was there,
And, as you might say, saw the lady born.
Paul worked at anything in lumbering.
He'd been hard at it taking boards away
For—I forget—the last ambitious sawyer
To want to find out if he couldn't pile

The lumber on Paul till Paul begged for mercy.
They'd sliced the first slab off a big butt log,
And the sawyer had slammed the carriage back
To slam end on again against the saw teeth.
To judge them by the way they caught themselves
When they saw what had happened to the log,
They must have had a guilty expectation
Something was going to go with their slambanging.
Something had left a broad black streak of grease
On the new wood the whole length of the log
Except, perhaps, a foot at either end.
But when Paul put his finger in the grease,
It wasn't grease at all, but a long slot.
The log was hollow. They were sawing pine.
"First time I ever saw a hollow pine.
That comes of having Paul around the place.
Take it to hell for me," the sawyer said.
Everyone had to have a look at it,

And tell Paul what he ought to do about it.
(They treated it as his.) "You take a jack-knife,
And spread the opening, and you've got a dug-out
All dug to go a-fishing in." To Paul
The hollow looked too sound and clean and empty
Ever to have housed birds or beasts or bees.
There was no entrance for them to get in by.
It looked to him like some new kind of hollow
He thought he'd *better* take his jack-knife to.
So after work that evening he came back
And let enough light into it by cutting
To see if it was empty. He made out in there
A slender length of pith, or was it pith?
It might have been the skin a snake had cast
And left stood up on end inside the tree
The hundred years the tree must have been growing.
More cutting and he had this in both hands,
And, looking from it to the pond near by,

43

Paul wondered how it would respond to water.
Not a breeze stirred, but just the breath of air
He made in walking slowly to the beach
Blew it once off his hands and almost broke it.
He laid it at the edge where it could drink.
At the first drink it rustled and grew limp.
At the next drink it grew invisible.
Paul dragged the shallows for it with his fingers,
And thought it must have melted. It was gone.
And then beyond the open water, dim with midges,
Where the log drive lay pressed against the boom,
It slowly rose a person, rose a girl,
Her wet hair heavy on her like a helmet,
Who, leaning on a log looked back at Paul.
And that made Paul in turn look back
To see if it was anyone behind him
That she was looking at instead of him.
Murphy had been there watching all the time,
But from a shed where neither of them could see him.
There was a moment of suspense in birth
When the girl seemed too water-logged to live,
Before she caught her first breath with a gasp
And laughed. Then she climbed slowly to her feet,
And walked off talking to herself or Paul
Across the logs like backs of alligators,
Paul taking after her around the pond.

Next evening Murphy and some other fellows
Got drunk, and tracked the pair up Catamount,
From the bare top of which there is a view
To other hills across a kettle valley.
And there, well after dark, let Murphy tell it,

They saw Paul and his creature keeping house.
It was the only glimpse that anyone
Has had of Paul and her since Murphy saw them
Falling in love across the twilight mill-pond.
More than a mile across the wilderness
They sat together half-way up a cliff
In a small niche let into it, the girl
Brightly, as if a star played on the place,
Paul darkly, like her shadow. All the light
Was from the girl herself, though, not from a star,
As was apparent from what happened next.
All those great ruffians put their throats together,
And let out a loud yell, and threw a bottle,
As a brute tribute of respect to beauty.
Of course the bottle fell short by a mile,
But the shout reached the girl and put her light out.
She went out like a firefly, and that was all.

So there were witnesses that Paul was married,
And not to anyone to be ashamed of.
Everyone had been wrong in judging Paul.
Murphy told me Paul put on all those airs
About his wife to keep her to himself.
Paul was what's called a terrible possessor.
Owning a wife with him meant owning her.
She wasn't anybody else's business,
Either to praise her, or so much as name her,
And he'd thank people not to think of her.
Murphy's idea was that a man like Paul
Wouldn't be spoken to about a wife
In any way the world knew how to speak.

Several interesting contrasts may be found in "Ghost House" and "The Witch of Coös" (page 33). Both are poems about ghosts. The first is a lyric; the second is a dramatic narrative. The first tells its experience in the poet's own terms; the second is told in the grim conversation of a woman whose son cannot stop her memories but tries to stop her from telling the whole truth. It is not hard to guess which poem was written in Frost's youth and which was composed in his forties.

GHOST HOUSE

I dwell in a lonely house I know
That vanished many a summer ago,
  And left no trace but the cellar walls,
  And a cellar in which the daylight falls,
And the purple-stemmed wild raspberries grow.

O'er ruined fences the grape-vines shield
The woods come back to the mowing field;
  The orchard tree has grown one copse
  Of new wood and old where the woodpecker chops;
The footpath down to the well is healed.

I dwell with a strangely aching heart
In that vanished abode there far apart
  On that disused and forgotten road
  That has no dust-bath now for the toad.
Night comes; the black bats tumble and dart;

The whippoorwill is coming to shout
And hush and cluck and flutter about:
  I hear him begin far enough away
  Full many a time to say his say
Before he arrives to say it out.

It is under the small, dim, summer star.
I know not who these mute folk are
  Who share the unlit place with me—
  Those stones out under the low-limbed tree
Doubtless bear names that the mosses mar.

They are tireless folk, but slow and sad,
Though two, close-keeping, are lass and lad—
    With none among them that ever sings,
    And yet, in view of how many things,
As sweet companions as might be had.

"At Woodward's Gardens" and "The Vindictives" are the sort of stories which Frost tells with such relish: stories that are also parables. "At Woodward's Gardens" takes us to a zoo. Had the Greek Aesop or the French La Fontaine told it, it might have been entitled, "The Boy, the Monkeys, and the Burning-Glass." But the fable is no less a fable because it has the American accents of the twentieth century, and its "moral" is as significant as any ancient sermon:

It's knowing what to do with things that counts.

AT WOODWARD'S GARDENS

A boy, presuming on his intellect,
Once showed two little monkeys in a cage
A burning-glass they could not understand
And never could be made to understand.
Words are no good: to say it was a lens
For gathering solar rays would not have helped.
But let him show them how the weapon worked.
He made the sun a pin-point on the nose
Of first one then the other till it brought
A look of puzzled dimness to their eyes
That blinking could not seem to blink away.
They stood arms laced together at the bars,
And exchanged troubled glances over life.
One put a thoughtful hand up to his nose
As if reminded—or as if perhaps
Within a million years of an idea.
He got his purple little knuckles stung.
The already known had once more been confirmed
By psychological experiment,
And that were all the finding to announce
Had the boy not presumed too close and long.
There was a sudden flash of arm, a snatch,
And the glass was the monkeys' not the boy's.
Precipitately they retired back cage
And instituted an investigation
On their part, though without the needed insight.
They bit the glass and listened for the flavor.
They broke the handle and the binding off it.
Then none the wiser, frankly gave it up,

And having hid it in their bedding straw
Against the day of prisoners' ennui,
Came dryly forward to the bars again
To answer for themselves: Who said it mattered
What monkeys did or didn't understand?
They might not understand a burning-glass.
They might not understand the sun itself.
It's knowing what to do with things that counts.

"The Vindictives" is a more biting parable. We are not
told the actual time and place, but there are enough refer-
ences in the poem to indicate that the background is Peru
at the time of the Spanish conquest. As in many of Frost's
poems, the event merges into meditation and prompts an
epigram which is also a lesson.

> . . . find what the hated need,
> Never mind of what actual worth,
> And wipe that out of the earth.
> Let them die of unsatisfied greed.

In such lines Frost appears to be a moralist, but his is a
new kind of didactic verse. It has simple beginnings, but it
arrives at strange conclusions. It is a poetry that is highly
personal and, at the same time, general. Yet the generalities
are not vague but sharp. Casual, straightforward, they are
somehow surprising.

You like to hear about gold.
A king filled his prison room
As full as the room could hold
To the top of his reach on the wall
With every known shape of the stuff.
'Twas to buy himself off his doom.
But it wasn't ransom enough.
His captors accepted it all,
But didn't let go of the king.
They made him send out a call
To his subjects to gather them more.
And his subjects wrung all they could wring
Out of temple and palace and store.
But when there seemed no more to bring,
His captors convicted the king
Of once having started a war,
And strangled the wretch with a string.

But really that gold was not half
That a king might have hoped to compel—
Not a half, not a third, not a tithe.
The king had scarce ceased to writhe,
When hate gave a terrible laugh,
Like a manhole opened to Hell.
If gold pleased the conqueror, well,
That gold should be the one thing
The conqueror henceforth should lack.

They gave no more thought to the king.
All joined in the game of hide-gold.
They swore all the gold should go back

Deep into the earth whence it came.
Their minds ran on cranny and crack.
All joined in the maddening game.
The tale is still boastingly told
Of many a treasure by name
That vanished into the black
And put out its light for the foe.

That self-sack and self-overthrow,
That was the splendidest sack
Since the forest Germans sacked Rome
And took the gold candlesticks home.

One Inca prince on the rack,
And late in his last hour alive,
Told them in what lake to dive
To seek what they seemed so to want.
They dived and nothing was found.
He told them to dive till they drowned.
The whole fierce conquering pack
Hunted and tortured and raged.
There were suns of story and vaunt
They searched for into Brazil
Their tongues hanging out unassuaged.

But the conquered grew meek and still.
They slowly and silently aged.
They kept their secrets and died,
Maliciously satisfied.
One knew of a burial hole
In the floor of a tribal cave,
Where under deep ash and charcoal
And cracked bones, human and beast,

The midden of feast upon feast,
Was coiled in its last resting grave.
The great treasure wanted the most,
The great thousand-linked gold chain,
Each link of a hundred weight,
That once between post and post
(In-leaning under the strain),
And looped ten times back and forth,
Had served as a palace gate.
Some said it had gone to the coast,
Some over the mountains east,
Some into the country north,
On the backs of a single-file host,
Commanded by one sun-priest,
And raising a dust with a train
Of flashing links in the sun.
No matter what some may say.
(The saying is never done.)
There bright in the filth it lay
Untarnished by rust and decay.
And be all plunderers curst.

"The best way to hate is the worst.
'Tis to find what the hated need,
Never mind of what actual worth,
And wipe that out of the earth.
Let them die of unsatisfied greed,
Of unsatisfied love of display,
Of unsatisfied love of the high,
Unvulgar, unsoiled, and ideal.
Let their trappings be taken away.
Let them suffer starvation and die
Of being brought down to the real."

"Wild Grapes" is another poem which is half-story, half-philosophy. This time it is a girl talking—a girl who talks in Robert Frost's tone of voice. The opening lines are something of a jest and something of a challenge.

> What tree may not the fig be gathered from?
> The grape may not be gathered from the birch?
> It's all you know the grape, or know the birch.

And so, without dropping the half-earnest, half-bantering manner, the poem proceeds to its story, dips into sheer humor, lifts itself into a study of character, and ends on a high note of faith and courage.

> I had not taken the first step in knowledge;
> I had not learned to let go with the hands,
> As still I have not learned to with the heart,
> And have no wish to with the heart, nor need
> That I can see. The mind—is not the heart.

Such poetry is not only personally revealing, it is a revelation of the American spirit, a spirit which refuses to expose its depths and hides its essential seriousness in a smile.

WILD GRAPES

What tree may not the fig be gathered from?
The grape may not be gathered from the birch?
It's all you know the grape, or know the birch.
As a girl gathered from the birch myself
Equally with my weight in grapes, one autumn,
I ought to know what tree the grape is fruit of.
I was born, I suppose, like anyone,
And grew to be a little boyish girl
My brother could not always leave at home.
But that beginning was wiped out in fear
The day I swung suspended with the grapes,
And was come after like Eurydice
And brought down safely from the upper regions;
And the life I live now's an extra life
I can waste as I please on whom I please.
So if you see me celebrate two birthdays,
And give myself out as two different ages,
One of them five years younger than I look—

One day my brother led me to a glade
Where a white birch he knew of stood alone,
Wearing a thin head-dress of pointed leaves,
And heavy on her heavy hair behind,
Against her neck, an ornament of grapes.
Grapes, I knew grapes from having seen them last year.
One bunch of them, and there began to be
Bunches all round me growing in white birches,
The way they grew round Lief the Lucky's German;

Mostly as much beyond my lifted hands, though,
As the moon used to seem when I was younger,
And only freely to be had for climbing.

My brother did the climbing; and at first
Threw me down grapes to miss and scatter
And have to hunt for in sweet fern and hardhack;
Which gave him some time to himself to eat,
But not so much, perhaps, as a boy needed.
So then, to make me wholly self-supporting,
He climbed still higher and bent the tree to earth,
And put it in my hands to pick my own grapes.
"Here, take a tree-top, I'll get down another.
Hold on with all your might when I let go."
I said I had the tree. It wasn't true.
The opposite was true. The tree had me.
The minute it was left with me alone
It caught me up as if I were the fish
And it the fishpole. So I was translated
To loud cries from my brother of "Let go!
Don't you know anything, you girl? Let go!"
But I, with something of the baby grip
Acquired ancestrally in just such trees
When wilder mothers than our wildest now
Hung babies out on branches by the hands
To dry or wash or tan, I don't know which
(You'll have to ask an evolutionist)—
I held on uncomplainingly for life.
My brother tried to make me laugh to help me.
"What are you doing up there in those grapes?
Don't be afraid. A few of them won't hurt you.
I mean, they won't pick you if you don't them."

Much danger of my picking anything!
By that time I was pretty well reduced
To a philosophy of hang-and-let-hang.
"Now you know how it feels," my brother said,
"To be a bunch of fox-grapes, as they call them,
That when it thinks it has escaped the fox
By growing where it shouldn't—on a birch,
Where a fox wouldn't think to look for it—
And if he looked and found it, couldn't reach it—
Just then come you and I to gather it.
Only you have the advantage of the grapes
In one way: you have one more stem to cling by,
And promise more resistance to the picker."

One by one I lost off my hat and shoes,
And still I clung. I let my head fall back,
And shut my eyes against the sun, my ears
Against my brother's nonsense. "Drop," he said,
"I'll catch you in my arms. It isn't far."
(Stated in lengths of him it might not be.)
"Drop or I'll shake the tree and shake you down."
Grim silence on my part as I sank lower,
My small wrists stretching till they showed the banjo strings.
"Why, if she isn't serious about it!
Hold tight awhile till I think what to do.
I'll bend the tree down and let you down by it."
I don't know much about the letting down;
But once I felt ground with my stocking feet
And the world came revolving back to me,
I know I looked long at my curled-up fingers,
Before I straightened them and brushed the bark off.
My brother said: "Don't you weigh anything?"

Try to weigh something next time, so you won't
Be run off with by birch trees into space."

It wasn't my not weighing anything
So much as my not knowing anything—
My brother had been nearer right before.
I had not taken the first step in knowledge;
I had not learned to let go with the hands,
As still I have not learned to with the heart,
And have no wish to with the heart—nor need,
That I can see. The mind—is not the heart.
I may yet live, as I know others live,
To wish in vain to let go with the mind—
Of cares, at night, to sleep; but nothing tells me
That I need learn to let go with the heart.

"The Bearer of Evil Tidings" is one of Frost's few com-
plete departures from the native scene. It takes place in the
ancient Himalayas, remote in space and time. To empha-
size the sense of antiquity, the poet has cast his lines into
simple ballad-like stanzas, and the whole poem mounts
quietly to a climax of charm and sly humor.

THE BEARER OF EVIL TIDINGS

The bearer of evil tidings,
When he was halfway there,
Remembered that evil tidings
Were a dangerous thing to bear.

So when he came to the parting
Where one road led to the throne
And one went off to the mountains
And into the wild unknown,

He took the one to the mountains.
He ran through the Vale of Cashmere,
He ran through the rhododendrons
Till he came to the land of Pamir.

And there in a precipice valley
A girl of his age he met
Took him home to her bower,
Or he might be running yet.

She taught him her tribe's religion:
How ages and ages since
A princess en route from China
To marry a Persian prince

Had been found with child; and her army
Had come to a troubled halt.
And though a god was the father
And nobody else at fault,

It had seemed discreet to remain there
And neither go on nor back.
So they stayed and declared a village
There in the land of the Yak.

And the child that came of the princess
Established a royal line,

And his mandates were given heed to
Because he was born divine.

And that was why there were people
On one Himalayan shelf;
And the bearer of evil tidings
Decided to stay there himself.

At least he had this in common
With the race he chose to adopt:
They had both of them had their reasons
For stopping where they had stopped.

As for his evil tidings,
Belshazzar's overthrow,
Why hurry to tell Belshazzar
What soon enough he would know?

"The Fear" and "Snow" are two of Frost's most dramatic
poems. They might be transferred from the printed page to
the theatre with scarcely a stage direction; they have, in
fact, been performed as one-act plays. Both are pitched in
the key of action; both are superb achievements in suspense
and tension. "Snow" is all the more dramatic because of its
contrast between inner serenity and outer violence—Me-
serve's monologue about the leaf erect in the open book is
not only a poem complete in itself, but a piece of casual
symbolism which intensifies the entire situation.

THE FEAR

A lantern light from deeper in the barn
Shone on a man and woman in the door
And threw their lurching shadows on a house
Near by, all dark in every glossy window.
A horse's hoof pawed once the hollow floor,
And the back of the gig they stood beside
Moved in a little. The man grasped a wheel,
The woman spoke out sharply, "Whoa, stand still!
I saw it just as plain as a white plate,"
She said, "as the light on the dashboard ran
Along the bushes at the roadside—a man's face.
You *must* have seen it too."

                    "I didn't see it.
Are you sure—"

          "Yes, I'm sure!"

                         "—it was a face?"

"Joel, I'll have to look. I can't go in,
I can't, and leave a thing like that unsettled.
Doors locked and curtains drawn will make no difference.
I always have felt strange when we came home
To the dark house after so long an absence,

And the key rattled loudly into place
Seemed to warn someone to be getting out
At one door as we entered at another.
What if I'm right, and someone all the time—
Don't hold my arm!"

            "I say it's someone passing."

"You speak as if this were a travelled road.
You forget where we are. What is beyond
That he'd be going to or coming from
At such an hour of night, and on foot too?
What was he standing still for in the bushes?"

"It's not so very late—it's only dark.
There's more in it than you're inclined to say.
Did he look like—?"

         "He looked like anyone.
I'll never rest to-night unless I know.
Give me the lantern."

           "You don't want the lantern."

She pushed past him and got it for herself.

"You're not to come," she said. "This is my business.
If the time's come to face it, I'm the one
To put it the right way. He'd never dare—
Listen! He kicked a stone. Hear that, hear that!
He's coming towards us. Joel, *go* in—please.
Hark!—I don't hear **him** now. But please go in."

"In the first place you can't make me believe it's—"

"It is—or someone else he's sent to watch.
And now's the time to have it out with him
While we know definitely where he is.
Let him get off and he'll be everywhere
Around us, looking out of trees and bushes
Till I sha'n't dare to set a foot outdoors.
And I can't stand it. Joel, let me go!"

"But it's nonsense to think he'd care enough."

"You mean you couldn't understand his caring.
Oh, but you see he hadn't had enough—
Joel, I won't—I won't—I promise you.
We mustn't say hard things. You mustn't either."

"I'll be the one, if anybody goes!
But you give him the advantage with this light.
What couldn't he do to us standing here!
And if to see was what he wanted, why
He has seen all there was to see and gone."

He appeared to forget to keep his hold,
But advanced with her as she crossed the grass.

"What do you want?" she cried to all the dark.
She stretched up tall to overlook the light
That hung in both hands hot against her skirt.

"There's no one; so you're wrong," he said.

"There is.
What do you want?" she cried, and then herself
Was startled when an answer really came.

"Nothing." It came from well along the road.

She reached a hand to Joel for support:
The smell of scorching woollen made her faint.

"What are you doing round this house at night?"

"Nothing." A pause: there seemed no more to say.

And then the voice again: "You seem afraid.
I saw by the way you whipped up the horse.
I'll just come forward in the lantern light
And let you see."

   "Yes, do.—Joel, go back!"

She stood her ground against the noisy steps
That came on, but her body rocked a little.

"You see," the voice said.

     "Oh." She looked and looked.

"You don't see—I've a child here by the hand.
A robber wouldn't have his family with him."

"What's a child doing at this time of night—?"

"Out walking. Every child should have the memory
Of at least one long-after-bedtime walk.
What, son?"

"Then I should think you'd try to find
Somewhere to walk—"

                    "The highway, as it happens—
We're stopping for the fortnight down at Dean's."

"But if that's all—Joel—you realize—
You won't think anything. You understand?
You understand that we have to be careful.
This is a very, very lonely place.
Joel." She spoke as if she couldn't turn.
The swinging lantern lengthened to the ground,
It touched, it struck, it clattered and went out.

SNOW

The three stood listening to a fresh access
Of wind that caught against the house a moment,
Gulped snow, and then blew free again—the Coles
Dressed, but dishevelled from some hours of sleep,
Meserve belittled in the great skin coat he wore.

Meserve was first to speak. He pointed backward
Over his shoulder with his pipe-stem, saying,
"You can just see it glancing off the roof
Making a great scroll upward toward the sky,

Long enough for recording all our names on.—
I think I'll just call up my wife and tell her
I'm here—so far—and starting on again.
I'll call her softly so that if she's wise
And gone to sleep, she needn't wake to answer."
Three times he barely stirred the bell, then listened.
"Why, Lett, still up? Lett, I'm at Cole's. I'm late.
I called you up to say Good-night from here
Before I went to say Good-morning there.—
I thought I would.—I know, but, Lett—I know—
I could, but what's the sense? The rest won't be
So bad.—Give me an hour for it.—Ho, ho,
Three hours to here! But that was all up hill;
The rest is down.—Why no, no, not a wallow:
They kept their heads and took their time to it
Like darlings, both of them. They're in the barn.—
My dear, I'm coming just the same. I didn't
Call you to ask you to invite me home.—"
He lingered for some word she wouldn't say,
Said it at last himself, "Good-night," and then
Getting no answer, closed the telephone.
The three stood in the lamplight round the table
With lowered eyes a moment till he said,
"I'll just see how the horses are."

                              "Yes, do."
Both the Coles said together. Mrs. Cole
Added: "You can judge better after seeing.—
I want you here with me, Fred. Leave him here,
Brother Meserve. You know to find your way
Out through the shed."

"I guess I know my way,
I guess I know where I can find my name
Carved in the shed to tell me who I am
If it don't tell me where I am. I used
To play—"

                "You tend your horses and come back.
Fred Cole, you're going to let him!"

                        "Well, aren't you?
How can you help yourself?"

                        "I called him Brother.
Why did I call him that?"

                        "It's right enough.
That's all you ever heard him called round here.
He seems to have lost off his Christian name."

"Christian enough I should call that myself.
He took no notice, did he? Well, at least
I didn't use it out of love of him,
The dear knows. I detest the thought of him
With his ten children under ten years old.
I hate his wretched little Racker Sect,
All's ever I heard of it, which isn't much.
But that's not saying—Look, Fred Cole, it's twelve,
Isn't it, now? He's been here half an hour.
He says he left the village store at nine.
Three hours to do four miles—a mile an hour
Or not much better. Why, it doesn't seem

As if a man could move that slow and move.
Try to think what he did with all that time.
And three miles more to go!"

                         "Don't let him go.
Stick to him, Helen. Make him answer you.
That sort of man talks straight on all his life
From the last thing he said himself, stone deaf
To anything anyone else may say.
I should have thought, though, you could make him hear
     you."

"What is he doing out a night like this?
Why can't he stay at home?"

                         "He had to preach."

"It's no night to be out."

                         "He may be small,
He may be good, but one thing's sure, he's tough."

"And strong of stale tobacco."

                         "He'll pull through."

"You only say so. Not another house
Or shelter to put into from this place
To theirs. I'm going to call his wife again."

"Wait and he may. Let's see what he will do.
Let's see if he will think of her again.

But then I doubt he's thinking of himself.
He doesn't look on it as anything."

"He shan't go—there!"

                    "It *is* a night, my dear."

"One thing: he didn't drag God into it."

"He don't consider it a case for God."

"You think so, do you? You don't know the kind.
He's getting up a miracle this minute.
Privately—to himself, right now, he's thinking
He'll make a case of it if he succeeds,
But keep still if he fails."

                    "Keep still all over.
He'll be dead—dead and buried."

                    "Such a trouble!
Not but I've every reason not to care
What happens to him if it only takes
Some of the sanctimonious conceit
Out of one of those pious scalawags."

"Nonsense to that! You want to see him safe."

"You like the runt."

              "Don't you a little?"

"Well,
I don't like what he's doing, which is what
You like, and like him for."

                    "Oh, yes you do.
You like your fun as well as anyone;
Only you women have to put these airs on
To impress men. You've got us so ashamed
Of being men we can't look at a good fight
Between two boys and not feel bound to stop it.
Let the man freeze an ear or two, I say.—
He's here. I leave him all to you. Go in
And save his life.—All right, come in, Meserve.
Sit down, sit down. How did you find the horses?"

"Fine, fine."

                    "And ready for some more? My wife here
Says it won't do. You've got to give it up."

"Won't you to please me? Please! If I say please?
Mr. Meserve, I'll leave it to *your* wife.
What *did* your wife say on the telephone?"

Meserve seemed to heed nothing but the lamp
Or something not far from it on the table.
By straightening out and lifting a forefinger,
He pointed with his hand from where it lay
Like a white crumpled spider on his knee:
"That leaf there in your open book! It moved
Just then, I thought. It's stood erect like that,
There on the table, ever since I came,

Trying to turn itself backward or forward,
I've had my eye on it to make out which;
If forward, then it's with a friend's impatience—
You see I know—to get you on to things
It wants to see how you will take, if backward
It's from regret for something you have passed
And failed to see the good of. Never mind,
Things must expect to come in front of us
A many times—I don't say just how many—
That varies with the things—before we see them.
One of the lies would make it out that nothing
Ever presents itself before us twice.
Where would we be at last if that were so?
Our very life depends on everything's
Recurring till we answer from within.
The thousandth time may prove the charm.—That leaf!
It can't turn either way. It needs the wind's help.
But the wind didn't move it if it moved.
It moved itself. The wind's at naught in here.
It couldn't stir so sensitively poised
A thing as that. It couldn't reach the lamp
To get a puff of black smoke from the flame,
Or blow a rumple in the collie's coat.
You make a little foursquare block of air,
Quiet and light and warm, in spite of all
The illimitable dark and cold and storm,
And by so doing give these three, lamp, dog,
And book-leaf, that keep near you, their repose;
Though for all anyone can tell, repose
May be the thing you haven't, yet you give it.
So false it is that what we haven't we can't give;
So false, that what we always say is true.

I'll have to turn the leaf if no one else will.
It won't lie down. Then let it stand. Who cares?"

"I shouldn't want to hurry you, Meserve,
But if you're going—Say you'll stay, you know.
But let me raise this curtain on a scene,
And show you how it's piling up against you.
You see the snow-white through the white of frost?
Ask Helen how far up the sash it's climbed
Since last we read the gage."

                        "It looks as if
Some pallid thing had squashed its features flat
And its eyes shut with overeagerness
To see what people found so interesting
In one another, and had gone to sleep
Of its own stupid lack of understanding,
Or broken its white neck of mushroom stuff
Short off, and died against the window-pane."

"Brother Meserve, take care, you'll scare yourself
More than you will us with such nightmare talk.
It's you it matters to, because it's you
Who have to go out into it alone."

"Let him talk, Helen, and perhaps he'll stay."

"Before you drop the curtain—I'm reminded:
You recollect the boy who came out here
To breathe the air one winter—had a room
Down at the Averys'? Well, one sunny morning
After a downy storm, he passed our place
And found me banking up the house with snow.

And I was burrowing in deep for warmth,
Piling it well above the window-sills.
The snow against the window caught his eye.
'Hey, that's a pretty thought'—those were his words.
'So you can think it's six feet deep outside,
While you sit warm and read up balanced rations.
You can't get too much winter in the winter.'
Those were his words. And he went home and all
But banked the daylight out of Avery's windows.
Now you and I would go to no such length.
At the same time you can't deny it makes
It not a mite worse, sitting here, we three,
Playing our fancy, to have the snowline run
So high across the pane outside. There where
There is a sort of tunnel in the frost
More like a tunnel than a hole—way down
At the far end of it you see a stir
And quiver like the frayed edge of the drift
Blown in the wind. I *like* that—I like *that*.
Well, now I leave you, people."

                         "Come, Meserve,
We thought you were deciding not to go—
The ways you found to say the praise of comfort
And being where you are. You want to stay."

"I'll own it's cold for such a fall of snow.
This house is frozen brittle, all except
This room you sit in. If you think the wind
Sounds further off, it's not because it's dying;
You're further under in the snow—that's all—
And feel it less. Hear the soft bombs of dust
It bursts against us at the chimney mouth,

And at the eaves. I like it from inside
More than I shall out in it. But the horses
Are rested and it's time to say good-night,
And let you get to bed again. Good-night,
Sorry I had to break in on your sleep."

"Lucky for you you did. Lucky for you
You had us for a half-way station
To stop at. If you were the kind of man
Paid heed to women, you'd take my advice
And for your family's sake stay where you are.
But what good is my saying it over and over?
You've done more than you had a right to think
You could do—*now*. You know the risk you take
In going on."

    "Our snow-storms as a rule
Aren't looked on as man-killers, and although
I'd rather be the beast that sleeps the sleep
Under it all, his door sealed up and lost,
Than the man fighting it to keep above it,
Yet think of the small birds at roost and not
In nests. Shall I be counted less than they are?
Their bulk in water would be frozen rock
In no time out to-night. And yet to-morrow
They will come budding boughs from tree to tree
Flirting their wings and saying Chickadee,
As if not knowing what you meant by the word storm."

"But why when no one wants you to go on?
Your wife—she doesn't want you to. We don't,
And you yourself don't want to. Who else is there?"

"Save us from being cornered by a woman.
Well, there's"—She told Fred afterward that in
The pause right there, she thought the dreaded word
Was coming, "God." But no, he only said
"Well, there's—the storm. That says I must go on.
That wants me as a war might if it came.
Ask any man."

        He threw her that as something
To last her till he got outside the door.
He had Cole with him to the barn to see him off.
When Cole returned he found his wife still standing
Beside the table near the open book,
Not reading it.

          "Well, what kind of a man
Do you call that?" she said.

           "He had the gift
Of words, or is it tongues, I ought to say?"

"Was ever such a man for seeing likeness?"

"Or disregarding people's civil questions—
What? We've found out in one hour more about him
Than we had seeing him pass by in the road
A thousand times. If that's the way he preaches!
You didn't think you'd keep him after all.
Oh, I'm not blaming you. He didn't leave you
Much say in the matter, and I'm just as glad
We're not in for a night of him. No sleep
If he had stayed. The least thing set him going.
It's quiet as an empty church without him."

"But how much better off are we as it is?
We'll have to sit here till we know he's safe."

"Yes, I suppose you'll want to, but I shouldn't.
He knows what he can do, or he wouldn't try.
Get into bed I say, and get some rest.
He won't come back, and if he telephones,
It won't be for an hour or two."

      "Well then.
We can't be any help by sitting here
And living his fight through with him, I suppose."

* * *

Cole had been telephoning in the dark.
Mrs. Cole's voice came from an inner room:
"Did she call you or you call her?"

       "She me.
You'd better dress: you won't go back to bed.
We must have been asleep: it's three and after."

"Had she been ringing long? I'll get my wrapper.
I want to speak to her."

      "All she said was,
He hadn't come and had he really started."

"She knew he had, poor thing, two hours ago."

"He had the shovel. He'll have made a fight."

"Why did I ever let him leave this house!"

"Don't begin that. You did the best you could
To keep him—though perhaps you didn't quite
Conceal a wish to see him show the spunk
To disobey you. Much his wife'll thank you."

"Fred, after all I said! You shan't make out
That it was any way but what it was.
Did she let on by any word she said
She didn't thank me?"

        "When I told her 'Gone,'
'Well then,' she said, and 'Well then'—like a threat.
And then her voice came scraping slow: 'Oh, you,
Why did you let him go?'"

        "Asked why we let him?
You let me there. I'll ask her why she let him.
She didn't dare to speak when he was here.
Their number's—twenty-one? The thing won't work.
Someone's receiver's down. The handle stumbles.
The stubborn thing, the way it jars your arm!
It's theirs. She's dropped it from her hand and gone."

"Try speaking. Say 'Hello!'"

        "Hello. Hello."

"What do you hear?"

        "I hear an empty room—
You know—it sounds that way. And yes, I hear—
I think I hear a clock—and windows rattling.
No step though. If she's there she's sitting down."

"Shout, she may hear you."

                        "Shouting is no good."

"Keep speaking then."

                    "Hello. Hello. Hello.
You don't suppose—? She wouldn't go out doors?"

"I'm half afraid that's just what she might do."

"And leave the children?"

                        "Wait and call again.
You can't hear whether she has left the door
Wide open and the wind's blown out the lamp
And the fire's died and the room's dark and cold?"

"One of two things, either she's gone to bed
Or gone out doors."

                        "In which case both are lost.
Do you know what she's like? Have you ever met her?
It's strange she doesn't want to speak to us."

                    "Fred, see if you can hear what I hear. Come."

"A clock maybe."

                        "Don't you hear something else?"

"Not talking."

"No."

      "Why, yes, I hear—what is it?"

"What do you say it is?"

        "A baby's crying!
Frantic it sounds, though muffled and far off.
Its mother wouldn't let it cry like that,
Not if she's there."

      "What do you make of it?"

"There's only one thing possible to make,
That is, assuming—that she has gone out.
Of course she hasn't though." They both sat down
Helpless. "There's nothing we can do till morning."

"Fred, I shan't let you think of going out."

"Hold on." The double bell began to chirp.
They started up. Fred took the telephone.
"Hello, Meserve. You're there, then!—And your wife?
Good! Why I asked—she didn't seem to answer.
He says she went to let him in the barn.—
We're glad. Oh, say no more about it, man.
Drop in and see us when you're passing."

      "Well,
She has him then, though what she wants him for
I *don't* see."

    "Possibly not for herself.

Maybe she only wants him for the children."

"The whole to-do seems to have been for nothing.
What spoiled our night was to him just his fun.
What did he come in for?—To talk and visit?
Thought he'd just call to tell us it was snowing.
If he thinks he is going to make our house
A half-way coffee house 'twixt town and nowhere—"

"I thought you'd feel you'd been too much concerned."

"You think you haven't been concerned yourself."

"If you mean he was inconsiderate
To rout us out to think for him at midnight
And then take our advice no more than nothing,
Why, I agree with you. But let's forgive him.
We've had a share in one night of his life.
What'll you bet he ever calls again?"

Some critics have found it difficult to see the constant hu-
mor in Frost; other critics, emphasizing the tragic side of
his work, have regretted the flickering wit, the capricious
"asides," the sheer fancifulness. Yet Frost is most profound
when he is most playful; no other poet has been so success-
ful in combining an outer lightness and an inner gravity.

"The Code" is a fine example of extremes: comedy and
near-tragedy; a frivolous, even farcical, episode that reveals
a deep philosophy. It is centered, like all of Frost's poems,
in experience and it dramatizes what every countryman
knows: a good hired man will let you tell him what to do
and when to do it. But, if you are wise, you won't tell him
how to do it!

80

THE CODE

There were three in the meadow by the brook
Gathering up windrows, piling cocks of hay,
With an eye always lifted toward the west
Where an irregular sun-bordered cloud
Darkly advanced with a perpetual dagger
Flickering across its bosom. Suddenly
One helper, thrusting pitchfork in the ground,
Marched himself off the field and home. One stayed.
The town-bred farmer failed to understand.

"What is there wrong?"

                              "Something you just now said."

"What did I say?"

                        "About our taking pains."

"To cock the hay?—because it's going to shower?
I said that more than half an hour ago.
I said it to myself as much as you."

"You didn't know. But James is one big fool.
He thought you meant to find fault with his work.
That's what the average farmer would have meant.
James would take time, of course, to chew it over
Before he acted: he's just got round to act."

"He is a fool if that's the way he takes me."

"Don't let it bother you. You've found out something.
The hand that knows his business won't be told
To do work better or faster—those two things.
I'm as particular as anyone:
Most likely I'd have served you just the same.
But I know you don't understand our ways.
You were just talking what was in your mind,
What was in all our minds, and you weren't hinting.
Tell you a story of what happened once:
I was up here in Salem at a man's
Named Sanders with a gang of four or five
Doing the haying. No one liked the boss.
He was one of the kind sports call a spider,
All wiry arms and legs that spread out wavy
From a humped body nigh as big's a biscuit.
But work! that man could work, especially
If by so doing he could get more work
Out of his hired help. I'm not denying

He was hard on himself. I couldn't find
That he kept any hours—not for himself.
Daylight and lantern-light were one to him:
I've heard him pounding in the barn all night.
But what he liked was someone to encourage.
Them that he couldn't lead he'd get behind
And drive, the way you can, you know, in mowing—
Keep at their heels and threaten to mow their legs off.
I'd seen about enough of his bulling tricks
(We call that bulling). I'd been watching him.
So when he paired off with me in the hayfield
To load the load, thinks I, Look out for trouble.
I built the load and topped it off; old Sanders
Combed it down with a rake and says 'O.K.'
Everything went well till we reached the barn
With a big jag to empty in a bay.
You understand that meant the easy job
For the man up on top of throwing *down*

The hay and rolling it off wholesale,
Where on a mow it would have been slow lifting.
You wouldn't think a fellow'd need much urging
Under those circumstances, would you now?
But the old fool seizes his fork in both hands,
And looking up bewhiskered out of the pit,
Shouts like an army captain, 'Let her come!'
Thinks I, D'ye mean it? 'What was that you said?'
I asked out loud, so's there'd be no mistake,
'Did you say, Let her come?' 'Yes, let her come.'
He said it over, but he said it softer.
Never you say a thing like that to a man,
Not if he values what he is. God, I'd as soon
Murdered him as left out his middle name.
I'd built the load and knew right where to find it.
Two or three forkfuls I picked lightly round for
Like meditating, and then I just dug in
And dumped the rackful on him in ten lots.
I looked over the side once in the dust
And caught sight of him treading-water-like,
Keeping his head above. 'Damn ye,' I says,
'That gets ye!' He squeaked like a squeezed rat.
That was the last I saw or heard of him.
I cleaned the rack and drove out to cool off.
As I sat mopping hayseed from my neck,
And sort of waiting to be asked about it,
One of the boys sings out, 'Where's the old man?'
'I left him in the barn under the hay.
If ye want him, ye can go and dig him out.'
They realized from the way I swobbed my neck
More than was needed something must be up.
They headed for the barn; I stayed where I was.
They told me afterward. First they forked hay,

A lot of it, out onto the barn floor.
Nothing! They listened for him. Not a rustle.
I guess they thought I'd spiked him in the temple
Before I buried him, or I couldn't have managed.
They excavated more. 'Go keep his wife
Out of the barn.' Someone looked in a window,
And curse me if he wasn't in the kitchen
Slumped way down in a chair, with both his feet
Against the stove, the hottest day that summer.
He looked so clean disgusted from behind
There was no one that dared to stir him up,
Or let him know that he was being looked at.
Apparently I hadn't buried him
(I may have knocked him down); but my just trying
To bury him had hurt his dignity.
He had gone to the house so's not to meet me.
He kept away from us all afternoon.
We tended to his hay. We saw him out
After a while picking peas in his garden:
He couldn't keep away from doing something."

"Weren't you relieved to find he wasn't dead?"

"No! and yet I don't know—it's hard to say.
I went about to kill him fair enough."

"You took an awkward way. Did he discharge you?"

"Discharge me? No! He knew I did just right."

III

THE HIRED MAN AND OTHER PEOPLE

The dedication of *North of Boston* speaks of the volume as "This book of people." And it is the people who dominate it—people questioning the purpose of a wall, differing about the meaning of "home," exposing themselves to ridiculous fears and the fear of ridicule, arguing about politics and mountain climbing and ancestors and law and housekeeping. But there is little anger and no violence even when the differences are most pronounced. There is banter in the disputes, and healing humor covers all.

It is the humor even more than the realism that distinguishes this poetry. Robert Frost is not a humorist in the sense of the comic-paper funmaker or the joking journalist.

His humor, like his truth-seeing, is in the main stream of native tradition. It is found in the earthy rather than in the bookish philosophers; in the serious, homespun American humorists and naturalists like Thoreau and Mark Twain. Such poems as "Brown's Descent" (page 103) and "To a Young Wretch" (page 124) and "The Cow in Apple Time" (page 217) are lyrics in which the laughter bubbles out of drollery. Other poems, such as "Two Tramps in Mud Time" (page 112) and "Fire and Ice" (page 242) and "Departmental": or, "The End of My Ant Jerry" (page 210) are perfect mixtures of quiet witticism and casual wisdom. The wisdom is all the more winning because the humor keeps it buoyant and serene, and sound at the core. Robert Frost wins us, as Wilfrid Wilson Gibson wrote in the poem quoted on page 17, by

> . . . shrewd turns and racy quips,
> And the rare twinkle of his grave blue eyes.

"Birches," one of Robert Frost's most widely quoted poems, beautifully illustrates the poet's power: the power to blend observation and imagination. It begins in the tone of easy conversation:

> When I see birches bend to left and right
> Across the lines of straighter darker trees . . .

And then, without warning or change of tone, the reader is arrested by a whimsical image, and the fact turns into a fancy:

> I like to think some boy's been swinging them.

Fact and fancy play together throughout the poem. The crystal ice becomes heaps of broken glass: "You'd think the inner dome of heaven had fallen." The arched trees are transformed into girls on hands and knees "that throw their hair before them over their heads to dry in the sun." The country boy, "whose only play was what he found himself," riding and subduing his father's birches, becomes the mature poet who announces:

> . . . Earth's the right place for love:
> I don't know where it's likely to go better.

Thus wisdom and whimsey join to make a poem that delights the mind and endears itself to the heart. The popularity of "Birches" lies in its combination of picture and human appeal. It is all the more appealing because of the shrewd turns and the "rare twinkle."

BIRCHES

When I see birches bend to left and right
Across the lines of straighter darker trees,
I like to think some boy's been swinging them.
But swinging doesn't bend them down to stay.
Ice-storms do that. Often you must have seen them
Loaded with ice a sunny winter morning
After a rain. They click upon themselves
As the breeze rises, and turn many-colored
As the stir cracks and crazes their enamel.
Soon the sun's warmth makes them shed crystal shells
Shattering and avalanching on the snow-crust—
Such heaps of broken glass to sweep away
You'd think the inner dome of heaven had fallen.
They are dragged to the withered bracken by the load,
And they seem not to break; though once they are bowed
So low for long, they never right themselves:
You may see their trunks arching in the woods
Years afterwards, trailing their leaves on the ground
Like girls on hands and knees that throw their hair
Before them over their heads to dry in the sun.
But I was going to say when Truth broke in
With all her matter-of-fact about the ice-storm
I should prefer to have some boy bend them
As he went out and in to fetch the cows—
Some boy too far from town to learn baseball,
Whose only play was what he found himself,
Summer or winter, and could play alone.

One by one he subdued his father's trees
By riding them down over and over again
Until he took the stiffness out of them,
And not one but hung limp, not one was left
For him to conquer. He learned all there was
To learn about not launching out too soon
And so not carrying the tree away
Clear to the ground. He always kept his poise
To the top branches, climbing carefully
With the same pains you use to fill a cup
Up to the brim, and even above the brim.
Then he flung outward, feet first, with a swish,
Kicking his way down through the air to the ground.
So was I once myself a swinger of birches.
And so I dream of going back to be.
It's when I'm weary of considerations,
And life is too much like a pathless wood
Where your face burns and tickles with the cobwebs
Broken across it, and one eye is weeping
From a twig's having lashed across it open.
I'd like to get away from earth awhile
And then come back to it and begin over.
May no fate willfully misunderstand me
And half grant what I wish and snatch me away
Not to return. Earth's the right place for love:
I don't know where it's likely to go better.
I'd like to go by climbing a birch tree,
And climb black branches up a snow-white trunk
Toward heaven, till the tree could bear no more,
But dipped its top and set me down again.
That would be good both going and coming back.
One could do worse than be a swinger of birches.

"Mowing" is a sonnet that reads like a lyric. It is one of Frost's early poems, but the tone is already mature, and the spirit is the spirit of the later work. The poet as laborer identifies himself with his scythe; and as the man and his instrument perform their task, their "earnest love" brings them to a simple and profound truth:

The fact is the sweetest dream that labor knows.

"Birches" assured the reader that "Earth's the right place for love." "For love—and labor, too," adds the scythe, whispering to the ground.

MOWING

There was never a sound beside the wood but one,
And that was my long scythe whispering to the ground.
What was it it whispered? I knew not well myself;
Perhaps it was something about the heat of the sun,
Something, perhaps, about the lack of sound—
And that was why it whispered and did not speak.
It was no dream of the gift of idle hours,
Or easy gold at the hand of fay or elf:
Anything more than the truth would have seemed too weak
To the earnest love that laid the swale in rows,
Not without feeble-pointed spikes of flowers
(Pale orchises), and scared a bright green snake.
The fact is the sweetest dream that labor knows.
My long scythe whispered and left the hay to make.

The strength of "Mending Wall," one of Frost's most often quoted poems, rests upon a contradiction. Its two famous lines oppose each other. The poem maintains that:

Something there is that doesn't love a wall.

But it also insists:

Good fences make good neighbours.

The contradiction is logical, for the opposing statements are uttered by two different types of people—and both are right. Man cannot live without walls, boundaries, limits and particularly self-limitations; yet he resents all bonds and is happy at the downfall of any barrier. In "Mending Wall" the boundary line is useless:

> There where it is we do not need the wall.

And, to emphasize the point, the speaker adds playfully:

> He is all pine and I am apple orchard.
> My apple trees will never get across
> And eat the cones under his pines, I tell him.

Some readers have found far-reaching implications in this poem. They have found that it states one of the greatest problems of our time: whether national walls should be made stronger for our protection, or whether they should be let down, since they cramp our progress toward understanding and eventual brotherhood. Other readers have read "Mending Wall" as a symbolic poem. In the voices of the two men—the younger, whimsical, "new-fashioned" speaker and the old-fashioned farmer who replies with his one determined sentence, his inherited maxim—some readers hear the clash of two forces: the spirit of revolt, which challenges tradition, and the spirit of restraint, which insists that conventions must be upheld, built up and continually rebuilt, as a matter of principle.

The poet himself frowns upon such symbolic interpretations. He denies that the poem says anything more than it seems to say. The contradiction is the heart of the poem. It answers itself in the paradox of people, in neighbors and competitors, in the contradictory nature of man.

MENDING WALL

Something there is that doesn't love a wall,
That sends the frozen-ground-swell under it,
And spills the upper boulders in the sun;
And makes gaps even two can pass abreast.
The work of hunters is another thing:
I have come after them and made repair
Where they have left not one stone on a stone,
But they would have the rabbit out of hiding,
To please the yelping dogs. The gaps I mean,
No one has seen them made or heard them made,
But at spring mending-time we find them there.
I let my neighbour know beyond the hill;
And on a day we meet to walk the line
And set the wall between us once again.
We keep the wall between us as we go.
To each the boulders that have fallen to each.
And some are loaves and some so nearly balls
We have to use a spell to make them balance:
"Stay where you are until our backs are turned!"
We wear our fingers rough with handling them.
Oh, just another kind of out-door game,
One on a side. It comes to little more:
There where it is we do not need the wall:
He is all pine and I am apple orchard.
My apple trees will never get across
And eat the cones under his pines, I tell him.
He only says, "Good fences make good neighbours."
Spring is the mischief in me, and I wonder
If I could put a notion in his head:

"*Why* do they make good neighbours? Isn't it
Where there are cows? But here there are no cows.
Before I built a wall I'd ask to know
What I was walling in or walling out,
And to whom I was like to give offence.
Something there is that doesn't love a wall,
That wants it down." I could say "Elves" to him,
But it's not elves exactly, and I'd rather
He said it for himself. I see him there
Bringing a stone grasped firmly by the top
In each hand, like an old-stone savage armed.
He moves in darkness as it seems to me,
Not of woods only and the shade of trees.
He will not go behind his father's saying,
And he likes having thought of it so well
He says again, "Good fences make good neighbours."

Frost triumphs not only in the contradictory aspects of man's spirit, but in the contrast of types of men. Three men are disclosed in "The Mountain," "Brown's Descent," and "The Vanishing Red," men who are typical in their very differences. There is the man in the first poem who is not impressed by the grandeur of the mountain; it is merely a wall behind which he is sheltered from the wind, a huge barrier preventing his village from growing: "That thing takes all the room!" He would not think of climbing it to see its strange brook, "always cold in summer, warm in winter"; he would consider it a waste of effort to climb it for the great view at the top; and to climb it for the sake of climbing would seem downright silly.

96

THE MOUNTAIN

The mountain held the town as in a shadow.
I saw so much before I slept there once:
I noticed that I missed stars in the west,
Where its black body cut into the sky.
Near me it seemed: I felt it like a wall
Behind which I was sheltered from a wind.
And yet between the town and it I found,
When I walked forth at dawn to see new things,
Were fields, a river, and beyond, more fields.
The river at the time was fallen away,
And made a widespread brawl on cobble-stones;
But the signs showed what it had done in spring:
Good grass-land gullied out, and in the grass
Ridges of sand, and driftwood stripped of bark.
I crossed the river and swung round the mountain.
And there I met a man who moved so slow
With white-faced oxen in a heavy cart,
It seemed no harm to stop him altogether.

"What town is this?" I asked.

                              "This? Lunenburg."

Then I was wrong: the town of my sojourn,
Beyond the bridge, was not that of the mountain,
But only felt at night its shadowy presence.
"Where is your village? Very far from here?"

"There is no village—only scattered farms.
We were but sixty voters last election.

We can't in nature grow to many more:
That thing takes all the room!" He moved his goad.
The mountain stood there to be pointed at.
Pasture ran up the side a little way,
And then there was a wall of trees with trunks;
After that only tops of trees, and cliffs
Imperfectly concealed among the leaves.
A dry ravine emerged from under boughs
Into the pasture.

                    "That looks like a path.
Is that the way to reach the top from here?—
Not for this morning, but some other time:
I must be getting back to breakfast now."

"I don't advise your trying from this side.
There is no proper path, but those that *have*
Been up, I understand, have climbed from Ladd's.
That's five miles back. You can't mistake the place:
They logged it there last winter some way up.
I'd take you, but I'm bound the other way."

"You've never climbed it?"

                              "I've been on the sides,
Deer-hunting and trout-fishing. There's a brook
That starts up on it somewhere—I've heard say
Right on the top, tip-top—a curious thing.
But what would interest you about the brook,
It's always cold in summer, warm in winter.
One of the great sights going is to see
It steam in winter like an ox's breath,

Until the bushes all along its banks
Are inch-deep with the frosty spines and bristles—
You know the kind. Then let the sun shine on it!"

"There ought to be a view around the world
From such a mountain—if it isn't wooded
Clear to the top." I saw through leafy screens
Great granite terraces in sun and shadow,
Shelves one could rest a knee on getting up—
With depths behind him sheer a hundred feet;
Or turn and sit on and look out and down,
With little ferns in crevices at his elbow.

"As to that I can't say. But there's the spring,

Right on the summit, almost like a fountain.
That ought to be worth seeing."

                        "If it's there.
You never saw it?"

                    "I guess there's no doubt
About its being there. I never saw it.
It may not be right on the very top:
It wouldn't have to be a long way down
To have some head of water from above,
And a *good distance* down might not be noticed
By anyone who'd come a long way up.
One time I asked a fellow climbing it
To look and tell me later how it was."

"What did he say?"

                    "He said there was a lake
Somewhere in Ireland on a mountain top."

"But a lake's different. What about the spring?"

"He never got up high enough to see.
That's why I don't advise your trying this side.
He tried this side. I've always meant to go
And look myself, but you know how it is:
It doesn't seem so much to climb a mountain
You've worked around the foot of all your life.
What would I do? Go in my overalls,
With a big stick, the same as when the cows
Haven't come down to the bars at milking time?

Or with a shotgun for a stray black bear?
'Twouldn't seem real to climb for climbing it."

"I shouldn't climb it if I didn't want to—
Not for the sake of climbing. What's its name?"

"We call it Hor: I don't know if that's right."

"Can one walk around it? Would it be too far?"

"You can drive round and keep in Lunenburg,
But it's as much as ever you can do,
The boundary lines keep in so close to it.
Hor is the township, and the township's Hor—
And a few houses sprinkled round the foot,
Like boulders broken off the upper cliff,
Rolled out a little farther than the rest."

"Warm in December, cold in June, you say?"

"I don't suppose the water's changed at all.
You and I know enough to know it's warm
Compared with cold, and cold compared with warm.
But all the fun's in how you say a thing."

"You've lived here all your life?"

                                    "Ever since Hor
Was no bigger than a—" What, I did not hear.
He drew the oxen toward him with light touches
Of his slim goad on nose and offside flank,
Gave them their marching orders and was moving.

Compared with the unnamed countryman who scorns to ascend mountains, there is the happy-go-lucky Brown, who delights in sliding down them. Brown has humor, there can be no doubt of it. And he also has character, firm Yankee character. In Brown's headlong descent there is something madcap and ridiculous and yet determined: a tart New England version of "John Gilpin's Ride."

BROWN'S DESCENT

OR

THE WILLY-NILLY SLIDE

Brown lived at such a lofty farm
  That everyone for miles could see
His lantern when he did his chores
  In winter after half-past three.

And many must have seen him make
  His wild descent from there one night,
'Cross lots, 'cross walls, 'cross everything,
  Describing rings of lantern light.

Between the house and barn the gale
  Got him by something he had on
And blew him out on the icy crust
  That cased the world, and he was gone!

Walls were all buried, trees were few:
  He saw no stay unless he stove
A hole in somewhere with his heel.
  But though repeatedly he strove

And stamped and said things to himself,
  And sometimes something seemed to yield,
He gained no foothold, but pursued
  His journey down from field to field.

Sometimes he came with arms outspread
    Like wings, revolving in the scene
Upon his longer axis, and
    With no small dignity of mien.

Faster or slower as he chanced,
    Sitting or standing as he chose,
According as he feared to risk
    His neck, or thought to spare his clothes,

He never let the lantern drop.
    And some exclaimed who saw afar
The figures he described with it,
    "I wonder what those signals are

Brown makes at such an hour of night!
    He's celebrating something strange.
I wonder if he's sold his farm,
    Or been made Master of the Grange."

He reeled, he lurched, he bobbed, he checked;
    He fell and made the lantern rattle
(But saved the light from going out.)
    So half-way down he fought the battle,

Incredulous of his own bad luck.
    And then becoming reconciled
To everything, he gave it up
    And came down like a coasting child.

"Well—I—be—" that was all he said,
    As standing in the river road,
He looked back up the slippery slope
    (Two miles it was) to his abode.

Sometimes as an authority
  On motor-cars, I'm asked if I
Should say our stock was petered out,
  And this is my sincere reply:

Yankees are what they always were.
  Don't think Brown ever gave up hope
Of getting home again because
  He couldn't climb that slippery slope;

Or even thought of standing there
  Until the January thaw
Should take the polish off the crust.
  He bowed with grace to natural law,

And then went round it on his feet,
  After the manner of our stock;
Not much concerned for those to whom,
  At that particular time o'clock,

It must have looked as if the course
  He steered was really straight away
From that which he was headed for—
  Not much concerned for them, I say;

No more so than became a man—
  And politician at odd seasons.
I've kept Brown standing in the cold
  While I invested him with reasons;

But now he snapped his eyes three times;
  Then shook his lantern, saying, "Ile's
'Bout out!" and took the long way home
  By road, a matter of several miles.

The humor which plays through "Brown's Descent" takes a tragic turn in "The Vanishing Red." Even the title is grim, for the phrase which usually indicates the gradual decline of the Indian is employed here in a cruelly literal sense.

You know the people in Frost's poems by the style of their humor: mild and uproarious, talkative and taciturn. The poems are short; stripped, as one critic said, to the granite. You know these people by the very brevity of their speech. You know so much about them even though—or because—they have said so little.

THE VANISHING RED

He is said to have been the last Red Man
In Acton. And the Miller is said to have laughed—
If you like to call such a sound a laugh.
But he gave no one else a laugher's license.
For he turned suddenly grave as if to say,
"Whose business,—if I take it on myself,
Whose business—but why talk round the barn?—
When it's just that I hold with getting a thing done with."
You can't get back and see it as he saw it.
It's too long a story to go into now.
You'd have to have been there and lived it.
Then you wouldn't have looked on it as just a matter
Of who began it between the two races.

Some guttural exclamation of surprise
The Red Man gave in poking about the mill
Over the great big thumping shuffling mill-stone
Disgusted the Miller physically as coming
From one who had no right to be heard from.
"Come, John," he said, "you want to see the wheel pit?"

He took him down below a cramping rafter,
And showed him, through a manhole in the floor,
The water in desperate straits like frantic fish,
Salmon and sturgeon, lashing with their tails.
Then he shut down the trap door with a ring in it
That jangled even above the general noise,
And came up stairs alone—and gave that laugh,
And said something to a man with a meal-sack
That the man with the meal-sack didn't catch—then.
Oh, yes, he showed John the wheel pit all right.

"To the Thawing Wind," "A Lone Striker," and "Two Tramps in Mud Time" were written at widely different periods of Frost's life, yet they have at least one thing in common: they are, to a large extent, autobiographical. More than in most verses, here we are given glimpses of the author's activities, his direct response, his personal attitude. It is interesting to note, for example, that "To the Thawing Wind" is practically the only poem in which Frost refers to himself as a poet.

Thus the three poems offer three pictures of the man (and the poet) at different stages of his development. They are arranged chronologically.

TO THE THAWING WIND

Come with rain, O loud Southwester!
Bring the singer, bring the nester;
Give the buried flower a dream;
Make the settled snow-bank steam;
Find the brown beneath the white;
But whate'er you do to-night,
Bathe my window, make it flow,
Melt it as the ice will go;
Melt the glass and leave the sticks
Like a hermit's crucifix;
Burst into my narrow stall;
Swing the picture on the wall;
Run the rattling pages o'er;
Scatter poems on the floor;
Turn the poet out of door.

A LONE STRIKER

The swinging mill bell changed its rate
To tolling like the count of fate,
And though at that the tardy ran,
One failed to make the closing gate.
There was a law of God or man
That on the one who came too late

The gate for half an hour be locked,
His time be lost, his pittance docked.
He stood rebuked and unemployed.
The straining mill began to shake.
The mill, though many, many eyed,
Had eyes inscrutably opaque;
So that he couldn't look inside
To see if some forlorn machine
Was standing idle for his sake.
(He couldn't hope its heart would break.)

And yet he thought he saw the scene:
The air was full of dust of wool.
A thousand yarns were under pull,
But pull so slow, with such a twist,
All day from spool to lesser spool,
It seldom overtaxed their strength;
They safely grew in slender length.
And if one broke by any chance,
The spinner saw it at a glance.
The spinner still was there to spin.

That's where the human still came in.
Her deft hand showed with finger rings
Among the harp-like spread of strings.
She caught the pieces end to end
And, with a touch that never missed,
Not so much tied as made them blend.
Man's ingenuity was good.
He saw it plainly where he stood,
Yet found it easy to resist.

He knew another place, a wood,
And in it, tall as trees, were cliffs;
And if he stood on one of these,
'Twould be among the tops of trees,
Their upper branches round him wreathing,
Their breathing mingled with his breathing.
If—if he stood! Enough of ifs!
He knew a path that wanted walking;
He knew a spring that wanted drinking;
A thought that wanted further thinking;
A love that wanted re-renewing.
Nor was this just a way of talking
To save him the expense of doing.
With him it boded action, deed.

The factory was very fine;
He wished it all the modern speed.
Yet, after all, 'twas not divine,
That is to say, 'twas not a church.
He never would assume that he'd
Be any institution's need.
But he said then and still would say
If there should ever come a day
When industry seemed like to die
Because he left it in the lurch,
Or even merely seemed to pine
For want of his approval, why
Come get him—they knew where to search.

TWO TRAMPS IN MUD TIME

Out of the mud two strangers came
And caught me splitting wood in the yard.
And one of them put me off my aim
By hailing cheerily "Hit them hard!"
I knew pretty well why he dropped behind
And let the other go on a way.
I knew pretty well what he had in mind:
He wanted to take my job for pay.

Good blocks of beech it was I split,
As large around as the chopping block;
And every piece I squarely hit
Fell splinterless as a cloven rock.
The blows that a life of self-control
Spares to strike for the common good
That day, giving a loose to my soul,
I spent on the unimportant wood.

The sun was warm but the wind was chill.
You know how it is with an April day
When the sun is out and the wind is still,
You're one month on in the middle of May.
But if you so much as dare to speak,
A cloud comes over the sunlit arch,
A wind comes off a frozen peak,
And you're two months back in the middle of March.

A bluebird comes tenderly up to alight
And fronts the wind to unruffle a plume
His song so pitched as not to excite
A single flower as yet to bloom.
It is snowing a flake: and he half knew
Winter was only playing possum.
Except in color he isn't blue,
But he wouldn't advise a thing to blossom.

The water for which we may have to look
In summertime with a witching-wand,
In every wheelrut's now a brook,
In every print of a hoof a pond.
Be glad of water, but don't forget
The lurking frost in the earth beneath
That will steal forth after the sun is set
And show on the water its crystal teeth.

The time when most I loved my task
These two must make me love it more
By coming with what they came to ask.
You'd think I never had felt before
The weight of an ax-head poised aloft,
The grip on earth of outspread feet.
The life of muscles rocking soft
And smooth and moist in vernal heat.

Out of the woods two hulking tramps
(From sleeping God knows where last night,
But not long since in the lumber camps).
They thought all chopping was theirs of right.

Men of the woods and lumberjacks,
They judged me by their appropriate tool.
Except as a fellow handled an ax,
They had no way of knowing a fool.

Nothing on either side was said.
They knew they had but to stay their stay
And all their logic would fill my head:
As that I had no right to play
With what was another man's work for gain.
My right might be love but theirs was need.
And where the two exist in twain
Theirs was the better right—agreed.

But yield who will to their separation,
My object in living is to unite
My avocation and my vocation
As my two eyes make one in sight.
Only where love and need are one,
And the work is play for mortal stakes,
Is the deed ever really done
For Heaven and the future's sakes.

"Love and a Question" is a further proof that Robert Frost is not a narrowly realistic poet, or an idyllic "nature poet," or a poet who can be put in any particular category. "Love and a Question" has the eerie spell of some ancient legend. There are overtones of old ballads in such phrases as "he spoke the bridegroom fair," "and, for all burden, care," and "wished her heart in a case of gold and pinned with a silver pin."

The poem tells a story, or part of a story, but the reader is left to guess what actually happens. The setting is real enough—a country house, a man and his young bride, and a Stranger out of the night—but the atmosphere is uncanny. The Stranger, too, is something more than he seems; he is not merely a person but a portent: a figure of care and coming trouble. The poem ends, as the title indicates, with a question.

LOVE AND A QUESTION

A Stranger came to the door at eve,
　　And he spoke the bridegroom fair.
He bore a green-white stick in his hand,
　　And, for all burden, care.
He asked with the eyes more than the lips
　　For a shelter for the night,
And he turned and looked at the road afar
　　Without a window light.

The bridegroom came forth into the porch
　　With "Let us look at the sky,
And question what of the night to be,
　　Stranger, you and I."
The woodbine leaves littered the yard,
　　The woodbine berries were blue,
Autumn, yes, winter was in the wind;
　　"Stranger, I wish I knew."

Within, the bride in the dusk alone
　　Bent over the open fire,
Her face rose-red with the glowing coal
　　And the thought of her heart's desire.
The bridegroom looked at the weary road,
　　Yet saw but her within,
And wished her heart in a case of gold
　　And pinned with a silver pin.

The bridegroom thought it little to give
    A dole of bread, a purse,
A heartfelt prayer for the poor of God,
    Or for the rich a curse;
But whether or not a man was asked
    To mar the love of two
By harboring woe in the bridal house,
    The bridegroom wished he knew.

"An Old Man's Winter Night," unlike "Love and a Question," is all actuality. The mood is established by the first line:

All out of doors looked darkly in at him . . .

It is increased by the superb suggestion of:

What kept him from remembering the need
That brought him to that creaking room was age.

Finally the description and the atmosphere are combined; the mood becomes the man.

A light he was to no one but himself
Where now he sat, concerned with he knew what,
A quiet light, and then not even that.

Never has the loneliness of old age been more sensitively, and more accurately, pictured.

AN OLD MAN'S WINTER NIGHT

All out of doors looked darkly in at him
Through the thin frost, almost in separate stars,
That gathers on the pane in empty rooms.
What kept his eyes from giving back the gaze
Was the lamp tilted near them in his hand.
What kept him from remembering the need
That brought him to that creaking room was age.
He stood with barrels round him—at a loss.
And having scared the cellar under him
In clomping there, he scared it once again
In clomping off;—and scared the outer night,
Which has its sounds, familiar, like the roar
Of trees and crack of branches, common things,
But nothing so like beating on a box.
A light he was to no one but himself
Where now he sat, concerned with he knew what,
A quiet light, and then not even that.
He consigned to the moon, such as she was,
So late-arising, to the broken moon
As better than the sun in any case
For such a charge, his snow upon the roof,
His icicles along the wall to keep;
And slept. The log that shifted with a jolt
Once in the stove, disturbed him and he shifted,
And eased his heavy breathing, but still slept.
One aged man—one man—can't keep a house,
A farm, a countryside, or if he can,
It's thus he does it of a winter night.

Characters as diverse as can be imagined are portrayed in "The Gum-Gatherer," "The Investment," "The Figure in the Doorway," and "To a Young Wretch." The method of presenting them is as various as the characters themselves. Sometimes they walk leisurely into our consciousness like "The Gum-Gatherer," or trip lightly into our hearts like the youngster in "To a Young Wretch," or enter pathetically like the young couple in "The Investment," or flash suddenly into our vision like "The Figure in the Doorway," glimpsed by the poet from the window of a dining car while the train sped through the Ozarks.

These people live with increasing vividness: in the poet's lines and in the reader's memory. They are drawn with affection, but not with a blurring sentimentality. They lose neither their sweetness nor their vigor, for they are portrayed with an unpitying sympathy, a tender exactitude.

THE GUM-GATHERER

There overtook me and drew me in
To his down-hill, early-morning stride,
And set me five miles on my road
Better than if he had had me ride,
A man with a swinging bag for load
And half the bag wound round his hand.
We talked like barking above the din
Of water we walked along beside.
And for my telling him where I'd been
And where I lived in mountain land
To be coming home the way I was,
He told me a little about himself.
He came from higher up in the pass
Where the grist of the new-beginning brooks
Is blocks split off the mountain mass—
And hopeless grist enough it looks
Ever to grind to soil for grass.
(The way it is will do for moss.)
There he had built his stolen shack.

It had to be a stolen shack
Because of the fears of fire and loss
That trouble the sleep of lumber folk:
Visions of half the world burned black
And the sun shrunken yellow in smoke.
We know who when they come to town
Bring berries under the wagon seat,
Or a basket of eggs between their feet;
What this man brought in a cotton sack
Was gum, the gum of the mountain spruce.
He showed me lumps of the scented stuff
Like uncut jewels, dull and rough.
It comes to market golden brown;
But turns to pink between the teeth.

I told him this is a pleasant life
To set your breast to the bark of trees
That all your days are dim beneath,
And reaching up with a little knife,
To loose the resin and take it down
And bring it to market when you please.

THE INVESTMENT

Over back where they speak of life as staying
("You couldn't call it living, for it ain't"),
There was an old, old house renewed with paint,
And in it a piano loudly playing.

Out in the ploughed ground in the cold a digger,
Among the unearthed potatoes standing still,
Was counting winter dinners, one a hill,
With half an ear to the piano's vigor.

All that piano and new paint back there,
Was it some money suddenly come into?
Or some extravagance young love had been to?
Or old love on an impulse not to care—

Not to sink under being man and wife,
But get some color and music out of life?

THE FIGURE IN THE DOORWAY

The grade surmounted, we were riding high
Through level mountains nothing to the eye
But scrub oak, scrub oak and the lack of earth
That kept the oaks from getting any girth.
But as through the monotony we ran,
We came to where there was a living man.
His great gaunt figure filled his cabin door,
And had he fallen inward on the floor,
He must have measured to the further wall.
But we who passed were not to see him fall.
The miles and miles he lived from anywhere
Were evidently something he could bear.
He stood unshaken, and if grim and gaunt,
It was not necessarily from want.
He had the oaks for heating and for light.
He had a hen, he had a pig in sight.
He had a well, he had the rain to catch.
He had a ten by twenty garden patch.
Nor did he lack for common entertainment.
That I assume was what our passing train meant.
He could look at us in our diner eating,
And if so moved uncurl a hand in greeting.

TO A YOUNG WRETCH

As gay for you to take your father's axe
As take his gun—rod—to go hunting—fishing.
You nick my spruce until its fiber cracks,
It gives up standing straight and goes down swishing.
You link an arm in its arm, and you lean
Across the light snow homeward smelling green.

I could have bought you just as good a tree
To frizzle resin in a candle flame,
And what a saving 'twould have meant to me.
But tree by charity is not the same
As tree by enterprise and expedition.
I must not spoil your Christmas with contrition.

It is your Christmases against my woods.
But even where thus opposing interests kill,
They are to be thought of as opposing goods
Oftener than as conflicting good and ill;
Which makes the war-god seem no special dunce
For always fighting on both sides at once.

And though in tinsel chain and popcorn rope,
My tree a captive in your window bay
Has lost its footing on my mountain slope
And lost the stars of heaven, may, oh, may
The symbol star it lifts against your ceiling
Help me accept its fate with Christmas feeling.

"The Wood-Pile" was singled out by Amy Lowell, poet and critic, because of its "absolute fidelity to fact." Many of the lines justify her, for they are bare of image-making and speculation, stripped clean of everything except perfect observation.

> It was a cord of maple, cut and split
> And piled—and measured, four by four by eight.
> And not another like it could I see.
> No runner tracks in this year's snow looped near it.
> And it was older sure than this year's cutting,
> Or even last year's or the year's before.

But the poet cannot be satisfied with "absolute fidelity to fact." The fact must be illuminated; and so, a few lines later, the age and condition of the woodpile are intensified by a brief but vivid simile:

>   . . . Clematis
> Had wound strings round and round it like a bundle.

In the heightened description of a woodpile, a person emerges. The reader sees him, a man careless and confident, always turning to something new, willing to forget the results of heavy labor; leaving the pile of logs

> To warm the frozen swamp as best it could
> With the slow smokeless burning of decay.

THE WOOD-PILE

Out walking in the frozen swamp one grey day,
I paused and said, "I will turn back from here.
No, I will go on farther—and we shall see."
The hard snow held me, save where now and then
One foot went through. The view was all in lines
Straight up and down of tall slim trees
Too much alike to mark or name a place by
So as to say for certain I was here
Or somewhere else: I was just far from home.

A small bird flew before me. He was careful
To put a tree between us when he lighted,
And say no word to tell me who he was
Who was so foolish as to think what *he* thought.
He thought that I was after him for a feather—
The white one in his tail; like one who takes
Everything said as personal to himself.
One flight out sideways would have undeceived him.
And then there was a pile of wood for which
I forgot him and let his little fear
Carry him off the way I might have gone,
Without so much as wishing him good-night.
He went behind it to make his last stand.
It was a cord of maple, cut and split
And piled—and measured, four by four by eight.
And not another like it could I see.
No runner tracks in this year's snow looped near it.
And it was older sure than this year's cutting,
Or even last year's or the year's before.
The wood was grey and the bark warping off it
And the pile somewhat sunken. Clematis
Had wound strings round and round it like a bundle.
What held it though on one side was a tree
Still growing, and on one a stake and prop,
These latter about to fall. I thought that only
Someone who lived in turning to fresh tasks
Could so forget his handiwork on which
He spent himself, the labour of his axe,
And leave it there far from a useful fireplace
To warm the frozen swamp as best it could
With the slow smokeless burning of decay.

The men in "A Hundred Collars" and "The Star-Splitter" are different in trade and training: a traveling newspaper man and a hit-or-miss farmer. Yet both men are visionaries. The collector for the newspaper may tipple and talk a little too much—a New Englander, for a change, who is anything but tight-lipped—yet he has a dream of this earth. The whole landscape comes to life as the loquacious Lafe expands in reminiscence:

> What I like best's the lay of different farms,
> Coming out on them from a stretch of woods,
> Or over a hill or round a sudden corner.
> I like to find the folks getting out in spring,
> Raking the dooryard, working near the house.
> Later they get out further in the fields. . . .
> The fields are stripped to lawn, the garden patches
> Stripped to bare ground, the maple trees
> To whips and poles. . . .

Brad McLaughlin, in "The Star-Splitter," is less concerned with earth and more with heaven. He is too curious about "our place among the infinities." Having burned down his farmhouse for the fire insurance, he puts the proceeds in a telescope; for he maintains

> The best thing that we're put here for's to see;
> The strongest thing that's given us to see with's
> A telescope. . . .

What unites both men still further is their unfailing humor: Lafe giving away his collars because he can't stop growing; Brad burning himself out of house and farm at one stroke (of a match, Frost reminds us) because he can't stop turning failure into philosophy.

A HUNDRED COLLARS

Lancaster bore him—such a little town,
Such a great man. It doesn't see him often
Of late years, though he keeps the old homestead
And sends the children down there with their mother
To run wild in the summer—a little wild.
Sometimes he joins them for a day or two
And sees old friends he somehow can't get near.
They meet him in the general store at night,
Pre-occupied with formidable mail,
Riffling a printed letter as he talks.
They seem afraid. He wouldn't have it so:
Though a great scholar, he's a democrat,
If not at heart, at least on principle.
Lately when coming up to Lancaster,
His train being late, he missed another train
And had four hours to wait at Woodsville Junction
After eleven o'clock at night. Too tired
To think of sitting such an ordeal out,
He turned to the hotel to find a bed.

"No room," the night clerk said. "Unless—"

Woodsville's a place of shrieks and wandering lamps
And cars that shock and rattle—and *one* hotel.

"You say 'Unless.'"

"Unless you wouldn't mind
Sharing a room with someone else."

"Who is it?"

"A man."

"So I should hope. What kind of man?"

"I know him: he's all right. A man's a man.
Separate beds, of course, you understand."
The night clerk blinked his eyes and dared him on.

"Who's that man sleeping in the office chair?
Has he had the refusal of my chance?"

"He was afraid of being robbed or murdered.
What do you say?"

"I'll have to have a bed."

The night clerk led him up three flights of stairs
And down a narrow passage full of doors,
At the last one of which he knocked and entered.
"Lafe, here's a fellow wants to share your room."

"Show him this way. I'm not afraid of him.
I'm not so drunk I can't take care of myself."

The night clerk clapped a bedstead on the foot.
"This will be yours. Good-night," he said, and went.

"Lafe was the name, I think?"

                              "Yes, *Lay*fayette.
You got it the first time. And yours?"

                                   "Magoon.
Doctor Magoon."

               "A Doctor?"

                              "Well, a teacher."

"Professor Square-the-circle-till-you're-tired?
Hold on, there's something I don't think of now
That I had on my mind to ask the first
Man that knew anything I happened in with.
I'll ask you later—don't let me forget it."

The Doctor looked at Lafe and looked away.
A man? A brute. Naked above the waist,
He sat there creased and shining in the light,
Fumbling the buttons in a well-starched shirt.
"I'm moving into a size-larger shirt.
I've felt mean lately; mean's no name for it.
I just found what the matter was to-night:
I've been a-choking like a nursery tree
When it outgrows the wire band of its name tag.

I blamed it on the hot spell we've been having.
'Twas nothing but my foolish hanging back,
Not liking to own up I'd grown a size.
Number eighteen this is. What size do you wear?"

The Doctor caught his throat convulsively.
"Oh—ah—fourteen—fourteen."

                     "Fourteen! You say so!
I can remember when I wore fourteen.
And come to think I must have back at home
More than a hundred collars, size fourteen.
Too bad to waste them all. You ought to have them.
They're yours and welcome; let me send them to you.
What makes you stand there on one leg like that?
You're not much furtherer than where Kike left you.
You act as if you wished you hadn't come.
Sit down or lie down, friend; you make me nervous."

The Doctor made a subdued dash for it,
And propped himself at bay against a pillow.

"Not that way, with your shoes on Kike's white bed.
You can't rest that way. Let me pull your shoes off."

"Don't touch me, please—I say, don't touch me, please.
I'll not be put to bed by you, my man."

"Just as you say. Have it your own way then.
'My man' is it? You talk like a professor.

Speaking of who's afraid of who, however,
I'm thinking I have more to lose than you
If anything should happen to be wrong.
Who wants to cut your number fourteen throat!
Let's have a show down as an evidence
Of good faith. There is ninety dollars.
Come, if you're not afraid."

                      "I'm not afraid.
There's five: that's all I carry."

                          "I can search you?
Where are you moving over to? Stay still.
You'd better tuck your money under you
And sleep on it the way I always do
When I'm with people I don't trust at night."

"Will you believe me if I put it there
Right on the counterpane—that I do trust you?"

"You'd say so, Mister Man.—I'm a collector.
My ninety isn't mine—you won't think that.
I pick it up a dollar at a time
All round the country for the *Weekly News*,
Published in Bow. You know the *Weekly News*?"

"Known it since I was young."

                        "Then you know me.
Now we are getting on together—talking.

I'm sort of Something for it at the front.
My business is to find what people want:
They pay for it, and so they ought to have it.
Fairbanks, he says to me—he's editor—
'Feel out the public sentiment'—he says.
A good deal comes on me when all is said.
The only trouble is we disagree
In politics: I'm Vermont Democrat—
You know what that is, sort of double-dyed;
The *News* has always been Republican.
Fairbanks, he says to me, 'Help us this year,'
Meaning by us their ticket. 'No,' I says,
'I can't and won't. You've been in long enough:
It's time you turned around and boosted us.
You'll have to pay me more than ten a week
If I'm expected to elect Bill Taft.
I doubt if I could do it anyway.' "

"You seem to shape the paper's policy."

"You see I'm in with everybody, know 'em all.
I almost know their farms as well as they do."

"You drive around? It must be pleasant work."

"It's business, but I can't say it's not fun.
What I like best's the lay of different farms,
Coming out on them from a stretch of woods,
Or over a hill or round a sudden corner.
I like to find folks getting out in spring,
Raking the dooryard, working near the house.

Later they get out further in the fields.
Everything's shut sometimes except the barn;
The family's all away in some back meadow.
There's a hay load a-coming—when it comes.
And later still they all get driven in:
The fields are stripped to lawn, the garden patches
Stripped to bare ground, the maple trees
To whips and poles. There's nobody about.
The chimney, though, keeps up a good brisk smoking.
And I lie back and ride. I take the reins
Only when someone's coming, and the mare
Stops when she likes: I tell her when to go.
I've spoiled Jemima in more ways than one.
She's got so she turns in at every house
As if she had some sort of curvature,
No matter if I have no errand there.
She thinks I'm sociable. I maybe am.
It's seldom I get down except for meals, though.
Folks entertain me from the kitchen doorstep,
All in a family row down to the youngest."

"One would suppose they might not be as glad
To see you as you are to see them."

                              "Oh,
Because I want their dollar? I don't want
Anything they've not got. I never dun.
I'm there, and they can pay me if they like.
I go nowhere on purpose: I happen by.
Sorry there is no cup to give you a drink.
I drink out of the bottle—not your style.

Mayn't I offer you—?"

                "No, no, no, thank you."

"Just as you say. Here's looking at you then.—
And now I'm leaving you a little while.
You'll rest easier when I'm gone, perhaps—
Lie down—let yourself go and get some sleep.
But first—let's see—what was I going to ask you?
Those collars—who shall I address them to,
Suppose you aren't awake when I come back?"

"Really, friend, I can't let you. You—may need them."

"Not till I shrink, when they'll be out of style."

"But really I—I have so many collars."

"I don't know who I rather would have have them.
They're only turning yellow where they are.
But you're the doctor as the saying is.
I'll put the light out. Don't you wait for me:
I've just begun the night. You get some sleep.
I'll knock so-fashion and peep round the door
When I come back so you'll know who it is.
There's nothing I'm afraid of like scared people.
I don't want you should shoot me in the head.
What am I doing carrying off this bottle?
There now, you get some sleep."

                    He shut the door.
The Doctor slid a little down the pillow.

THE STAR-SPLITTER

"You know Orion always comes up sideways.
Throwing a leg up over our fence of mountains,
And rising on his hands, he looks in on me
Busy outdoors by lantern-light with something
I should have done by daylight, and indeed,
After the ground is frozen, I should have done
Before it froze, and a gust flings a handful
Of waste leaves at my smoky lantern chimney
To make fun of my way of doing things,
Or else fun of Orion's having caught me.
Has a man, I should like to ask, no rights
These forces are obliged to pay respect to?"
So Brad McLaughlin mingled reckless talk
Of heavenly stars with hugger-mugger farming,
Till having failed at hugger-mugger farming,
He burned his house down for the fire insurance
And spent the proceeds on a telescope
To satisfy a life-long curiosity
About our place among the infinities.
"What do you want with one of those blame things?"
I asked him well beforehand. "Don't you get one!"
"Don't call it blamed; there isn't anything
More blameless in the sense of being less
A weapon in our human fight," he said.
"I'll have one if I sell my farm to buy it."

There where he moved the rocks to plow the ground
And plowed between the rocks he couldn't move,
Few farms changed hands; so rather than spend years
Trying to sell his farm and then not selling,
He burned his house down for the fire insurance
And bought the telescope with what it came to.
He had been heard to say by several:
"The best thing that we're put here for's to see;
The strongest thing that's given us to see with's
A telescope. Someone in every town
Seems to me owes it to the town to keep one.
In Littleton it may as well be me."
After such loose talk it was no surprise
When he did what he did and burned his house down.

Mean laughter went about the town that day
To let him know we weren't the least imposed on,
And he could wait—we'd see to him to-morrow.
But the first thing next morning we reflected
If one by one we counted people out
For the least sin, it wouldn't take us long
To get so we had no one left to live with.
For to be social is to be forgiving.
Our thief, the one who does our stealing from us,
We don't cut off from coming to church suppers,
But what we miss we go to him and ask for.
He promptly gives it back, that is if still
Uneaten, unworn out, or undisposed of.
It wouldn't do to be too hard on Brad
About his telescope. Beyond the age
Of being given one's gift for Christmas,
He had to take the best way he knew how

To find himself in one. Well, all we said was
He took a strange thing to be roguish over.
Some sympathy was wasted on the house,
A good old-timer dating back along;
But a house isn't sentient; the house
Didn't feel anything. And if it did,
Why not regard it as a sacrifice,
And an old-fashioned sacrifice by fire,
Instead of a new-fashioned one at auction?

Out of a house and so out of a farm
At one stroke (of a match), Brad had to turn
To earn a living on the Concord railroad,
As under-ticket-agent at a station
Where his job, when he wasn't selling tickets,
Was setting out up track and down, not plants
As on a farm, but planets, evening stars
That varied in their hue from red to green.

He got a good glass for six hundred dollars.
His new job gave him leisure for star-gazing.
Often he bid me come and have a look
Up the brass barrel, velvet black inside,
At a star quaking in the other end.
I recollect a night of broken clouds
And underfoot snow melted down to ice,
And melting further in the wind to mud.
Bradford and I had out the telescope.
We spread our two legs as we spread its three,
Pointed our thoughts the way we pointed it,
And standing at our leisure till the day broke,
Said some of the best things we ever said.

That telescope was christened the Star-splitter,
Because it didn't do a thing but split
A star in two or three the way you split
A globule of quicksilver in your hand
With one stroke of your finger in the middle.
It's a star-splitter if there ever was one
And ought to do some good if splitting stars
'Sa thing to be compared with splitting wood.

We've looked and looked, but after all where are we?
Do we know any better where we are,
And how it stands between the night to-night
And a man with a smoky lantern chimney?
How different from the way it ever stood?

·   ·   ·

Humor and anguish are evenly balanced in "The House-keeper." Here again, as in the best of Frost, the surcharged atmosphere is increased and, at the same time, lightened by the casual tone of voice. Here is a domestic drama in which four ordinary people are involved; and yet the central figure, the extraordinary one, does not disclose her mind. Although she is fully realized, she does not even appear.

THE HOUSEKEEPER

I let myself in at the kitchen door.

"It's you," she said. "I can't get up. Forgive me
Not answering your knock. I can no more
Let people in than I can keep them out.
I'm getting too old for my size, I tell them.
My fingers are about all I've the use of
So's to take any comfort. I can sew:
I help out with this beadwork what I can."

"That's a smart pair of pumps you're beading there.
Who are they for?"

                    "You mean?—oh, for some miss.
I can't keep track of other people's daughters.
Lord, if I were to dream of everyone
Whose shoes I primped to dance in!"

                              "And where's John?"

"Haven't you seen him? Strange what set you off
To come to his house when he's gone to yours.
You can't have passed each other. I know what:
He must have changed his mind and gone to Garland's.
He won't be long in that case. You can wait.
Though what good you can be, or anyone—

It's gone so far. You've heard? Estelle's run off."

"Yes, what's it all about? When did she go?"

"Two weeks since."

"She's in earnest, it appears."

"I'm sure she won't come back. She's hiding somewhere.
I don't know where myself. John thinks I do.
He thinks I only have to say the word,
And she'll come back. But, bless you, I'm her mother—
I can't talk to her, and, Lord, if I could!"

"It will go hard with John. What will he do?
He can't find anyone to take her place."

"Oh, if you ask me that, what *will* he do?
He gets some sort of bakeshop meals together,
With me to sit and tell him everything,
What's wanted and how much and where it is.
But when I'm gone—of course I can't stay here:
Estelle's to take me when she's settled down.
He and I only hinder one another.
I tell them they can't get me through the door, though:
I've been built in here like a big church organ.
We've been here fifteen years."

"That's a long time
To live together and then pull apart.

How do you see him living when you're gone?
Two of you out will leave an empty house."

"I don't just see him living many years,
Left here with nothing but the furniture.
I hate to think of the old place when we're gone,
With the brook going by below the yard,
And no one here but hens blowing about.
If he could sell the place, but then, he can't:
No one will ever live on it again.
It's too run down. This is the last of it.
What I think he will do, is let things smash.
He'll sort of swear the time away. He's awful!
I never saw a man let family troubles
Make so much difference in his man's affairs.
He's just dropped everything. He's like a child.
I blame his being brought up by his mother.
He's got hay down that's been rained on three times.
He hoed a little yesterday for me:
I thought the growing things would do him good.
Something went wrong. I saw him throw the hoe
Sky-high with both hands. I can see it now—
Come here—I'll show you—in that apple tree.
That's no way for a man to do at his age:
He's fifty-five, you know, if he's a day."

"Aren't you afraid of him? What's that gun for?"

"Oh, that's been there for hawks since chicken-time.
John Hall touch me! Not if he knows his friends.
I'll say that for him, John's no threatener

Like some men folk. No one's afraid of him;
All is, he's made up his mind not to stand
What he has got to stand."

                    "Where is Estelle?
Couldn't one talk to her? What does she say?
You say you don't know where she is."

                                   "Nor want to!
She thinks if it was bad to live with him,
It must be right to leave him."

                         "Which is wrong!"

"Yes, but he should have married her."

                                   "I know."

"The strain's been too much for her all these years:
I can't explain it any other way.
It's different with a man, at least with John:
He knows he's kinder than the run of men.
Better than married ought to be as good
As married—that's what he has always said.
I know the way he's felt—but all the same!"

"I wonder why he doesn't marry her
And end it."

                    "Too late now: she wouldn't have him.
He's given her time to think of something else.
That's his mistake. The dear knows my interest

Has been to keep the thing from breaking up.
This is a good home: I don't ask for better.
But when I've said, 'Why shouldn't they be married,'
He'd say, 'Why should they?' no more words than that."

"And after all why should they? John's been fair
I take it. What was his was always hers.
There was no quarrel about property."

"Reason enough, there was no property.
A friend or two as good as own the farm,
Such as it is. It isn't worth the mortgage."

"I mean Estelle has always held the purse."

"The rights of that are harder to get at.
I guess Estelle and I have filled the purse.
'Twas we let him have money, not he us.
John's a bad farmer. I'm not blaming him.
Take it year in, year out, he doesn't make much.
We came here for a home for me, you know,
Estelle to do the housework for the board
Of both of us. But look how it turns out:
She seems to have the housework, and besides
Half of the outdoor work, though as for that,
He'd say she does it more because she likes it.
You see our pretty things are all outdoors.
Our hens and cows and pigs are always better
Than folks like us have any business with.
Farmers around twice as well off as we
Haven't as good. They don't go with the farm.

One thing you can't help liking about John,
He's fond of nice things—too fond, some would say.
But Estelle don't complain: she's like him there.
She wants our hens to be the best there are.
You never saw this room before a show,
Full of lank, shivery, half-drowned birds
In separate coops, having their plumage done.
The smell of the wet feathers in the heat!
You spoke of John's not being safe to stay with.
You don't know what a gentle lot we are:
We wouldn't hurt a hen! You ought to see us
Moving a flock of hens from place to place.
We're not allowed to take them upside down,
All we can hold together by the legs.
Two at a time's the rule, one on each arm,
No matter how far and how many times
We have to go."

                "You mean that's John's idea."

"And we live up to it; or I don't know
What childishness he wouldn't give way to.
He manages to keep the upper hand
On his own farm. He's boss. But as to hens:
We fence our flowers in and the hens range.
Nothing's too good for them. We say it pays.
John likes to tell the offers he has had,
Twenty for this cock, twenty-five for that.
He never takes the money. If they're worth
That much to sell, they're worth as much to keep.
Bless you, it's all expense, though. Reach me down

The little tin box on the cupboard shelf,
The upper shelf, the tin box. That's the one.
I'll show you. Here you are."

                    "What's this?"

                              "A bill—
For fifty dollars for one Langshang cock—
Receipted. And the cock is in the yard."

"Not in a glass case, then?"

                    "He'd need a tall one:
He can eat off a barrel from the ground.
He's been in a glass case, as you may say,
The Crystal Palace, London. He's imported.
John bought him, and we paid the bill with beads—
Wampum, I call it. Mind, we don't complain.
But you see, don't you, we take care of him."

"And like it, too. It makes it all the worse."

"It seems as if. And that's not all: he's helpless
In ways that I can hardly tell you of.
Sometimes he gets possessed to keep accounts
To see where all the money goes so fast.
You know how men will be ridiculous.
But it's just fun the way he gets bedeviled—
If he's untidy now, what will he be—?"

"It makes it all the worse. You must be blind."

"Estelle's the one. You needn't talk to me."

"Can't you and I get to the root of it?
What's the real trouble? What will satisfy her?"

"It's as I say: she's turned from him, that's all."

"But why, when she's well off? Is it the neighbours,
Being cut off from friends?"

                    "We have our friends.
That isn't it. Folks aren't afraid of us."

"She's let it worry her. You stood the strain,
And you're her mother."

                    "But I didn't always.
I didn't relish it along at first.
But I got wonted to it. And besides—
John said I was too old to have grandchildren.
But what's the use of talking when it's done?
She won't come back—it's worse than that—she can't."

"Why do you speak like that? What do you know?
What do you mean?—she's done harm to herself?"

"I mean she's married—married someone else."

"Oho, oho!"

"You don't believe me."

                              "Yes, I do,
Only too well. I knew there must be something!
So that was what was back. She's bad, that's all!"

"Bad to get married when she had the chance?"

"Nonsense! See what she's done! But who, but who—"

"Who'd marry her straight out of such a mess?
Say it right out—no matter for her mother.
The man was found. I'd better name no names.
John himself won't imagine who he is."

"Then it's all up. I think I'll get away.
You'll be expecting John. I pity Estelle;
I suppose she deserves some pity, too.
You ought to have the kitchen to yourself
To break it to him. You may have the job."

"You needn't think you're going to get away.
John's almost here. I've had my eye on someone
Coming down Ryan's Hill. I thought 'twas him.
Here he is now. This box! Put it away.
And this bill."

                    "What's the hurry? He'll unhitch."

"No, he won't, either. He'll just drop the reins
And turn Doll out to pasture, rig and all.

She won't get far before the wheels hang up
On something—there's no harm. See, there he is!
My, but he looks as if he must have heard!"

John threw the door wide but he didn't enter.
"How are you, neighbour? Just the man I'm after.
Isn't it Hell," he said. "I want to know.
Come out here if you want to hear me talk.
I'll talk to you, old woman, afterward.
I've got some news that maybe isn't news.
What are they trying to do to me, these two?"

"Do go along with him and stop his shouting."
She raised her voice against the closing door:
"Who wants to hear your news, you—dreadful fool?"

.   .   .

The five poems grouped as a sequence in "The Hill Wife"
form a remarkably rounded portrait of fear and love and
loneliness. The last poem ("The Impulse") seems an echo
of the unwed wife in "The Housekeeper," but the almost
painful sensitivity is outspoken when the wife declares her-
self in the first person in "Loneliness" and "The Smile." The
song-like quality of those lyrics makes the pathos all the
more poignant.

THE HILL WIFE

LONELINESS

(Her Word)

One ought not to have to care
   So much as you and I
Care when the birds come round the house
   To seem to say good-bye;

Or care so much when they come back
   With whatever it is they sing;
The truth being we are as much
   Too glad for the one thing

As we are too sad for the other here—
   With birds that fill their breasts
But with each other and themselves
   And their built or driven nests.

HOUSE FEAR

Always—I tell you this they learned—
Always at night when they returned
To the lonely house from far away
To lamps unlighted and fire gone gray,
They learned to rattle the lock and key
To give whatever might chance to be
Warning and time to be off in flight:

And preferring the out- to the in-door night,
They learned to leave the house-door wide
Until they had lit the lamp inside.

THE SMILE

(Her Word)

I didn't like the way he went away.
That smile! It never came of being gay.
Still he smiled—did you see him?—I was sure!
Perhaps because we gave him only bread
And the wretch knew from that that we were poor.
Perhaps because he let us give instead
Of seizing from us as he might have seized.
Perhaps he mocked at us for being wed,
Or being very young (and he was pleased
To have a vision of us old and dead).
I wonder how far down the road he's got.
He's watching from the woods as like as not.

THE OFT-REPEATED DREAM

She had no saying dark enough
    For the dark pine that kept
Forever trying the window-latch
    Of the room where they slept.

The tireless but ineffectual hands
    That with every futile pass
Made the great tree seem as a little bird
    Before the mystery of glass!

It never had been inside the room,
   And only one of the two
Was afraid in an oft-repeated dream
   Of what the tree might do.

THE IMPULSE

It was too lonely for her there,
   And too wild,
And since there were but two of them,
   And no child,

And work was little in the house,
   She was free,
And followed where he furrowed field,
   Or felled tree.

She rested on a log and tossed
   The fresh chips,
With a song only to herself
   On her lips.

And once she went to break a bough
   Of black alder.
She strayed so far she scarcely heard
   When he called her—

And didn't answer—didn't speak—
   Or return.
She stood, and then she ran and hid
   In the fern.

He never found her, though he looked
   Everywhere,
And he asked at her mother's house
   Was she there.

Sudden and swift and light as that
   The ties gave,
And he learned of finalities
   Besides the grave.

* * *

It has sometimes been said that Frost is reticent to the point of impersonality and that he has not given himself away in love poems. Nothing could be further from the truth. Frost, like all true poets, reveals himself in everything he writes, not only in his pictures of other people but in his self-portraits. Personal touches, quick and characteristic, illumine such love poems as "Going for Water," "Revelation," "A Line-Storm Song," and the lighter but no less lovely "The Telephone."

THE TELEPHONE

"When I was just as far as I could walk
From here to-day,
There was an hour
All still
When leaning with my head against a flower
I heard you talk.
Don't say I didn't, for I heard you say—
You spoke from that flower on the window sill—
Do you remember what it was you said?"

"First tell me what it was you thought you heard."

"Having found the flower and driven a bee away,
I leaned my head,
And holding by the stalk,
I listened and I thought I caught the word—
What was it? Did you call me by my name?
Or did you say—
Someone said 'Come'—I heard it as I bowed."

"I may have thought as much, but not aloud."

"Well, so I came."

REVELATION

We make ourselves a place apart
    Behind light words that tease and flout,
But oh, the agitated heart
    Till someone find us really out.

'Tis pity if the case require
    (Or so we say) that in the end
We speak the literal to inspire
    The understanding of a friend.

But so with all, from babes that play
    At hide-and-seek to God afar,
So all who hide too well away
    Must speak and tell us where they are.

GOING FOR WATER

The well was dry beside the door,
　And so we went with pail and can
Across the fields behind the house
　To seek the brook if still it ran;

Not loth to have excuse to go,
　Because the autumn eve was fair
(Though chill), because the fields were ours,
　And by the brook our woods were there.

We ran as if to meet the moon
　That slowly dawned behind the trees,
The barren boughs without the leaves,
　Without the birds, without the breeze.

But once within the wood, we paused
　Like gnomes that hid us from the moon,
Ready to run to hiding new
　With laughter when she found us soon.

Each laid on other a staying hand
　To listen ere we dared to look,
And in the hush we joined to make
　We heard, we knew we heard the brook.

A note as from a single place,
　A slender tinkling fall that made
Now drops that floated on the pool
　Like pearls, and now a silver blade.

A LINE-STORM SONG

The line-storm clouds fly tattered and swift,
  The road is forlorn all day,
Where a myriad snowy quartz stones lift,
  And the hoof-prints vanish away.
The roadside flowers, too wet for the bee,
  Expend their bloom in vain.
Come over the hills and far with me,
  And be my love in the rain.

The birds have less to say for themselves
  In the wood-world's torn despair
Than now these numberless years the elves,
  Although they are no less there:
All song of the woods is crushed like some
  Wild, easily shattered rose.
Come, be my love in the wet woods, come,
  Where the boughs rain when it blows.

There is the gale to urge behind
  And bruit our singing down,
And the shallow waters aflutter with wind
  From which to gather your gown.
What matter if we go clear to the west,
  And come not through dry-shod?
For wilding brooch shall wet your breast
  The rain-fresh goldenrod.

Oh, never this whelming east wind swells
  But it seems like the sea's return
To the ancient lands where it left the shells
  Before the age of the fern;

And it seems like the time when after doubt
  Our love came back amain.
Oh, come forth into the storm and rout
  And be my love in the rain.

. . .

"The Death of the Hired Man" is many kinds of poem. It is a narrative, a dialogue, a drama; it has been successfully acted as a one-act play. Three people are portrayed: a farmer, his wife, and an old incompetent hired hand, shiftless and proud—and the character most fully revealed is the one who never appears.

The poem has endeared itself to readers of every kind, and for many reasons. Some readers have praised it for its authentic power, its conversational beauty, its rich sense of ordinary life. Others have been won by its eloquent descriptions, particularly by such a passage as:

> Part of a moon was falling down the west,
> Dragging the whole sky with it to the hills.
> Its light poured softly in her lap. She saw it
> And spread her apron to it. She put out her hand
> Among the harp-like morning-glory strings,
> Taut with the dew from garden bed to eaves,
> As if she played unheard some tenderness
> That wrought on him beside her in the night.

Perhaps the most famous lines in the poem are those in which husband and wife trade definitions of home. Here the mood changes, and light irony is exchanged for deep pathos. The husband's mocking definition is offered first:

> "Home is the place where, when you have to go there,
> They have to take you in."

To which the wife, with a reproving mildness, replies:

> "I should have called it
> Something you somehow haven't to deserve."

"The Death of the Hired Man" is one of the most touching human episodes, the more so since it is all so quiet. The story unfolds itself in undertones; a poem heard—or overheard—in whispers.

THE DEATH OF THE HIRED MAN

Mary sat musing on the lamp-flame at the table
Waiting for Warren. When she heard his step,
She ran on tip-toe down the darkened passage
To meet him in the doorway with the news
And put him on his guard. "Silas is back."
She pushed him outward with her through the door
And shut it after her. "Be kind," she said.
She took the market things from Warren's arms
And set them on the porch, then drew him down
To sit beside her on the wooden steps.

"When was I ever anything but kind to him?
But I'll not have the fellow back," he said.
"I told him so last haying, didn't I?
'If he left then,' I said, 'that ended it.'
What good is he? Who else will harbour him
At his age for the little he can do?
What help he is there's no depending on.
Off he goes always when I need him most.
'He thinks he ought to earn a little pay,
Enough at least to buy tobacco with,
So he won't have to beg and be beholden.'
'All right,' I say, 'I can't afford to pay
Any fixed wages, though I wish I could.'
'Someone else can.' 'Then someone else will have to.'
I shouldn't mind his bettering himself
If that was what it was. You can be certain,
When he begins like that, there's someone at him
Trying to coax him off with pocket-money,—

In haying time, when any help is scarce.
In winter he comes back to us. I'm done."

"Sh! not so loud: he'll hear you," Mary said.

"I want him to: he'll have to soon or late."

"He's worn out. He's asleep beside the stove.
When I came up from Rowe's I found him here,
Huddled against the barn-door fast asleep,
A miserable sight, and frightening, too—
You needn't smile—I didn't recognize him—
I wasn't looking for him—and he's changed.
Wait till you see."

                    "Where did you say he'd been?"

"He didn't say. I dragged him to the house,
And gave him tea and tried to make him smoke.
I tried to make him talk about his travels.
Nothing would do: he just kept nodding off."

"What did he say? Did he say anything?"

"But little."

        "Anything? Mary, confess
He said he'd come to ditch the meadow for me."

"Warren!"

        "But did he? I just want to know."

"Of course he did. What would you have him say?
Surely you wouldn't grudge the poor old man
Some humble way to save his self-respect.
He added, if you really care to know,
He meant to clear the upper pasture, too.
That sounds like something you have heard before?
Warren, I wish you could have heard the way
He jumbled everything. I stopped to look
Two or three times—he made me feel so queer—
To see if he was talking in his sleep.
He ran on Harold Wilson—you remember—
The boy you had in haying four years since.
He's finished school, and teaching in his college.
Silas declares you'll have to get him back.
He says they two will make a team for work:
Between them they will lay this farm as smooth!
The way he mixed that in with other things.
He thinks young Wilson a likely lad, though daft
On education—you know how they fought
All through July under the blazing sun,
Silas up on the cart to build the load,
Harold along beside to pitch it on."

"Yes, I took care to keep well out of earshot."

"Well, those days trouble Silas like a dream.
You wouldn't think they would. How some things linger!
Harold's young college boy's assurance piqued him.
After so many years he still keeps finding
Good arguments he sees he might have used.
I sympathise. I know just how it feels
To think of the right thing to say too late.

Harold's associated in his mind with Latin.
He asked me what I thought of Harold's saying
He studied Latin like the violin
Because he liked it—that an argument!
He said he couldn't make the boy believe
He could find water with a hazel prong—
Which showed how much good school had ever done him.
He wanted to go over that. But most of all
He thinks if he could have another chance
To teach him how to build a load of hay—"

"I know, that's Silas' one accomplishment.
He bundles every forkful in its place,
And tags and numbers it for future reference,
So he can find and easily dislodge it
In the unloading. Silas does that well.
He takes it out in bunches like big birds' nests.
You never see him standing on the hay
He's trying to lift, straining to lift himself."

"He thinks if he could teach him that, he'd be
Some good perhaps to someone in the world.
He hates to see a boy the fool of books.
Poor Silas, so concerned for other folk,
And nothing to look backward to with pride,
And nothing to look forward to with hope,
So now and never any different."

Part of a moon was falling down the west,
Dragging the whole sky with it to the hills.
Its light poured softly in her lap. She saw it
And spread her apron to it. She put out her hand

Among the harp-like morning-glory strings,
Taut with the dew from garden bed to eaves,
As if she played unheard some tenderness
That wrought on him beside her in the night.
"Warren," she said, "he has come home to die:
You needn't be afraid he'll leave you this time."

"Home," he mocked gently.

"Yes, what else but home?
It all depends on what you mean by home.
Of course he's nothing to us, any more
Than was the hound that came a stranger to us
Out of the woods, worn out upon the trail."

"Home is the place where, when you have to go there,
They have to take you in."

                              "I should have called it
Something you somehow haven't to deserve."

Warren leaned out and took a step or two,
Picked up a little stick, and brought it back
And broke it in his hand and tossed it by.
"Silas has better claim on us you think
Than on his brother? Thirteen little miles
As the road winds would bring him to his door.
Silas has walked that far no doubt to-day.
Why didn't he go there? His brother's rich.
A somebody—director in the bank."

"He never told us that."

                    "We know it though."

"I think his brother ought to help, of course.
I'll see to that if there is need. He ought of right
To take him in, and might be willing to—
He may be better than appearances.
But have some pity on Silas. Do you think
If he had any pride in claiming kin
Or anything he looked for from his brother,
He'd keep so still about him all this time?"

"I wonder what's between them."

                              "I can tell you.
Silas is what he is—we wouldn't mind him—
But just the kind that kinsfolk can't abide.
He never did a thing so very bad.
He don't know why he isn't quite as good

As anybody. Worthless though he is,
He won't be made ashamed to please his brother."

"I can't think Si ever hurt anyone."

"No, but he hurt my heart the way he lay.
And rolled his old head on that sharp-edged chair-back.
He wouldn't let me put him on the lounge.
You must go in and see what you can do.
I made the bed up for him there to-night.
You'll be surprised at him—how much he's broken.
His working days are done; I'm sure of it."

"I'd not be in a hurry to say that."

"I haven't been. Go, look, see for yourself.
But, Warren, please remember how it is:
He's come to help you ditch the meadow.
He has a plan. You mustn't laugh at him.
He may not speak of it, and then he may.
I'll sit and see if that small sailing cloud
Will hit or miss the moon."

     It hit the moon.
Then there were three there, making a dim row,
The moon, the little silver cloud, and she.

Warren returned—too soon, it seemed to her,
Slipped to her side, caught up her hand and waited.

"Warren?" she questioned.

     "Dead," was all he answered.

IV

STOPPING BY WOODS
AND OTHER PLACES

The poems of Robert Frost have a way of uniting opposites. They are casual in tone but profound in effect, teasing and intense, playful yet deeply penetrating. Even when they seem to be about a particular place they suggest ideas unlimited by space.

This combination of the local and the universal is illustrated by "Hyla Brook," a poem that has the sound and the approximate shape of a sonnet. But the poet has gone beyond the pattern by adding a fifteenth line, and it is that line which caps the picture with clear and universal wisdom:

We love the things we love for what they are.

This is the highest form of affection. When seen with the eyes of love, the thin and almost dried-up brook is as winning as when the stream flashed with speed and sang with the spring song of young frogs ("the Hyla breed"), a brook beloved by those "who remember long."

HYLA BROOK

By June our brook's run out of song and speed.
Sought for much after that, it will be found
Either to have gone groping underground
(And taken with it all the Hyla breed
That shouted in the mist a month ago,
Like ghost of sleigh-bells in a ghost of snow)—
Or flourished and come up in jewel-weed,
Weak foliage that is blown upon and bent
Even against the way its waters went.
Its bed is left a faded paper sheet
Of dead leaves stuck together by the heat—
A brook to none but who remember long.
This as it will be seen is other far
Than with brooks taken otherwhere in song.
We love the things we love for what they are.

The title-poem of Frost's fifth volume, *West-running Brook*, is another study in contraries. It is a playful argument with a serious undertone, an extended bit of fooling that turns into a philosophy, teasing and tender, a dialogue that leads up to a memorable monologue. In the backward motion of the white wave running counter to itself, "the tribute of the current to the source," the poet sees the origin of all of us.

WEST-RUNNING BROOK

"Fred, where is north?"

                        "North? North is there, my love.
The brook runs west."

                       "West-running Brook then call it."
(West-running Brook men call it to this day.)
"What does it think it's doing running west
When all the other country brooks flow east
To reach the ocean? It must be the brook
Can trust itself to go by contraries
The way I can with you—and you with me—
Because we're—we're—I don't know what we are.
What are we?"

                  "Young or new?"

                        "We must be something.

We've said we two. Let's change that to we three.
As you and I are married to each other,
We'll both be married to the brook. We'll build
Our bridge across it, and the bridge shall be
Our arm thrown over it asleep beside it.
Look, look, it's waving to us with a wave
To let us know it hears me."

                "Why, my dear,
That wave's been standing off this jut of shore—"
(The black stream, catching on a sunken rock,
Flung backward on itself in one white wave,
And the white water rode the black forever,
Not gaining but not losing, like a bird
White feathers from the struggle of whose breast
Flecked the dark stream and flecked the darker pool
Below the point, and were at last driven wrinkled
In a white scarf against the far shore alders.)
"That wave's been standing off this jut of shore
Ever since rivers, I was going to say,
Were made in heaven. It wasn't waved to us."

"It wasn't, yet it was. If not to you
It was to me—in an annunciation."

"Oh, if you take it off to lady-land,
As't were the country of the Amazons
We men must see you to the confines of
And leave you there, ourselves forbid to enter,—
It is your brook! I have no more to say."

"Yes, you have, too. Go on. You thought of something."

"Speaking of contraries, see how the brook
In that white wave runs counter to itself.
It is from that in water we were from
Long, long before we were from any creature.
Here we, in our impatience of the steps,
Get back to the beginning of beginnings,
The stream of everything that runs away.
Some say existence like a Pirouot
And Pirouette, forever in one place,
Stands still and dances, but it runs away,
It seriously, sadly, runs away
To fill the abyss' void with emptiness.
It flows beside us in this water brook,
But it flows over us. It flows between us
To separate us for a panic moment.
It flows between us, over us, and *with* us.
And it is time, strength, tone, light, life and love—
And even substance lapsing unsubstantial;
The universal cataract of death
That spends to nothingness—and unresisted,
Save by some strange resistance in itself,
Not just a swerving, but a throwing back,
As if regret were in it and were sacred.
It has this throwing backward on itself
So that the fall of most of it is always
Raising a little, sending up a little.
Our life runs down in sending up the clock.
The brook runs down in sending up our life.
The sun runs down in sending up the brook.
And there is something sending up the sun.
It is this backward motion toward the source,
Against the stream, that most we see ourselves in,

The tribute of the current to the source.
It is from this in nature we are from.
It is most us."

      "Today will be the day
You said so."

      "No, today will be the day
You said the brook was called West-running Brook."

"Today will be the day of what we both said."

   .   .   .

Frost's poetry gives significance to seemingly insignificant
things and places: a patch of old snow in the shaded corner
of a field, a friend's horse standing in the road, a wintry
tree still holding last year's leaves, a lonely house at sunset,
a few feet of alder swamp.

A PATCH OF OLD SNOW

There's a patch of old snow in a corner
   That I should have guessed
Was a blow-away paper the rain
   Had brought to rest.

It is speckled with grime as if
   Small print overspread it,
The news of a day I've forgotten—
   If I ever read it.

A TIME TO TALK

When a friend calls to me from the road
And slows his horse to a meaning walk,
I don't stand still and look around
On all the hills I haven't hoed,
And shout from where I am, "What is it?"
No, not as there is a time to talk.
I thrust my hoe in the mellow ground,
Blade-end up and five feet tall,
And plod: I go up to the stone wall
For a friendly visit.

A BOUNDLESS MOMENT

He halted in the wind, and—what was that
Far in the maples, pale, but not a ghost?
He stood there bringing March against his thought,
And yet too ready to believe the most.

"Oh that's the Paradise-in-bloom," I said;
And truly it was fair enough for flowers
Had we but in us to assume in March
Such white luxuriance of May for ours.

We stood a moment so in a strange world,
Myself as one his own pretense deceives;
And then I said the truth (and we moved on).
A young beech clinging to its last year's leaves.

BEREFT

Where had I heard this wind before
Change like this to a deeper roar?
What would it take my standing there for,
Holding open a restive door,
Looking down hill to a frothy shore?
Summer was past and day was past.
Sombre clouds in the west were massed.
Out in the porch's sagging floor,
Leaves got up in a coil and hissed,
Blindly struck at my knee and missed.
Something sinister in the tone
Told me my secret must be known:
Word I was in the house alone
Somehow must have gotten abroad,
Word I was in my life alone,
Word I had no one left but God.

A WINTER EDEN

A winter garden in an alder swamp,
Where conies now come out to sun and romp,
As near a paradise as it can be
And not melt snow or start a dormant tree.

It lifts existence on a plane of snow
One level higher than the earth below,
One level nearer heaven overhead,
And last year's berries shining scarlet red.

It lifts a gaunt luxuriating beast
Where he can stretch and hold his highest feast
On some wild apple tree's young tender bark,
What well may prove the year's high girdle mark.

So near to paradise all pairing ends:
Here loveless birds now flock as winter friends,
Content with bud-inspecting. They presume
To say which buds are leaf and which are bloom.

A feather-hammer gives a double knock.
This Eden day is done at two o'clock.
An hour of winter day might seem too short
To make it worth life's while to wake and sport.

In certain villages, especially in small towns whose chief industry is fishing, it is not uncommon to see a rowboat or a deep-sea dory on some well-kept lawn. There, instead of being filled with fish, it is full of flowers.

The picture is incongruous and, at the same time, commonplace. But the poet does more than show its queerness, its combination of the strange and the familiar. He extends the vision of a flower-filled boat and the fantasy of one more journey into the unknown.

THE FLOWER BOAT

The fisherman's swapping a yarn for a yarn
Under the hand of the village barber,
And here in the angle of house and barn
His deep-sea dory has found a harbor.

At anchor she rides the sunny sod
As full to the gunnel of flowers growing
As ever she turned her home with cod
From George's bank when winds were blowing.

And I judge from that Elysian freight
That all they ask is rougher weather,
And dory and master will sail by fate
To seek for the Happy Isles together.

Robert Frost is much more than a descriptive poet. He finds as much in places as in people. The scene lives vividly in his poetry because it is crowded with the intimate human drama. The slab-built, paper-covered house a hundred miles from any other habitation ("The Census-Taker") prompts a yearning in the midst of nothingness:

It must be I want life to go on living.

Here the empty place is peopled with the past, and the business of living takes on fresh significance.

THE CENSUS-TAKER

I came an errand one cloud-blowing evening
To a slab-built, black-paper-covered house
Of one room and one window and one door,
The only dwelling in a waste cut over
A hundred square miles round it in the mountains:
And that not dwelt in now by men or women.
(It never had been dwelt in, though, by women,
So what is this I make a sorrow of?)
I came as census-taker to the waste
To count the people in it and found none,
None in the hundred miles, none in the house,
Where I came last with some hope, but not much
After hours' overlooking from the cliffs
An emptiness flayed to the very stone.
I found no people that dared show themselves,
None not in hiding from the outward eye.
The time was autumn, but how anyone
Could tell the time of year when every tree

That could have dropped a leaf was down itself
And nothing but the stump of it was left
Now bringing out its rings in sugar of pitch;
And every tree up stood a rotting trunk
Without a single leaf to spend on autumn,
Or branch to whistle after what was spent.
Perhaps the wind the more without the help
Of breathing trees said something of the time
Of year or day the way it swung a door
Forever off the latch, as if rude men
Passed in and slammed it shut each one behind him
For the next one to open for himself.
I counted nine I had no right to count
(But this was dreamy unofficial counting)
Before I made the tenth across the threshold.
Where was my supper? Where was anyone's?
No lamp was lit. Nothing was on the table.
The stove was cold—the stove was off the chimney,
And down by one side where it lacked a leg.
The people that had loudly passed the door
Were people to the ear but not the eye.
They were not on the table with their elbows.
They were not sleeping in the shelves of bunks.
I saw no men there and no bones of men there.
I armed myself against such bones as might be
With the pitch-blackened stub of an axe-handle
I picked up off the straw-dust covered floor.
Not bones, but the ill-fitted window rattled.
The door was still because I held it shut
While I thought what to do that could be done—
About the house—about the people not there.
This house in one year fallen to decay
Filled me with no less sorrow than the houses

Fallen to ruin in ten thousand years
Where Asia wedges Africa from Europe.
Nothing was left to do that I could see
Unless to find that there was no one there
And declare to the cliffs too far for echo,
"The place is desert and let whoso lurks
In silence, if in this he is aggrieved,
Break silence now or be forever silent.
Let him say why it should not be declared so."
The melancholy of having to count souls
Where they grow fewer and fewer every year
Is extreme where they shrink to none at all.
It must be I want life to go on living.

Change of scene brings a change of mood, but it is not
merely the scene that is depicted in this poetry. The trans-
formation of an old farmhouse into a city house is accen-
tuated by the decline of a brook into a sewer. Recalling
that "the world is too much with us," the poet wonders
whether such change must not be paid for, whether the
underground muttering of the debased stream might not:

. . . keep
This new-built city from both work and sleep.

A BROOK IN THE CITY

The farm house lingers, though averse to square
With the new city street it has to wear
A number in. But what about the brook
That held the house as in an elbow-crook?
I ask as one who knew the brook, its strength
And impulse, having dipped a finger length
And made it leap my knuckle, having tossed
A flower to try its currents where they crossed.
The meadow grass could be cemented down
From growing under pavements of a town;
The apple trees be sent to hearth-stone flame.
Is water wood to serve a brook the same?
How else dispose of an immortal force
No longer needed? Staunch it at its source
With cinder loads dumped down? The brook was thrown
Deep in a sewer dungeon under stone
In fetid darkness still to live and run—
And all for nothing it had ever done
Except forget to go in fear perhaps.
No one would know except for ancient maps
That such a brook ran water. But I wonder
If from its being kept forever under
The thoughts may not have risen that so keep
This new-built city from both work and sleep.

The poet is fascinated with shrunken brooks and expanding trees, with dark woods and bright beaches, with the wavelike shape of sand dunes and the way the snow disappears, leaving nothing white except:

> . . . here a birch,
> And there a clump of houses with a church.

The woods heavy with snow are not used merely as a setting, a depressing reminder of cold death. On the contrary, the poet speaks up for the undying solace of the stars ("Evening in a Sugar Orchard") and for the triumph of returning life ("The Onset"):

> I know that winter death has never tried
> The earth but it has failed: the snow may heap
> In long storms an undrifted four feet deep
> As measured against maple, birch and oak,
> It cannot check the peeper's silver croak . . .

The shifting earth in "Sand Dunes" is, seemingly, a place of hazard. Yet it is only another challenge to man, one more place to build and leave, so he may be:

> . . . more free to think
> For the one more cast off shell.

Even an unnamed tree, a "vague dream-head lifted out of the ground," in "Tree at My Window," participates in the life of those about it. It, too, shares in the moving human drama, "taken and swept and all but lost."

EVENING IN A SUGAR ORCHARD

From where I lingered in a lull in March
Outside the sugar-house one night for choice,
I called the fireman with a careful voice
And bade him leave the pan and stoke the arch:
"O fireman, give the fire another stoke,
And send more sparks up chimney with the smoke."
I thought a few might tangle, as they did,
Among bare maple boughs, and in the rare
Hill atmosphere not cease to glow,
And so be added to the moon up there.
The moon, though slight, was moon enough to show
On every tree a bucket with a lid,
And on black ground a bear-skin rug of snow.
The sparks made no attempt to be the moon.
They were content to figure in the trees
As Leo, Orion, and the Pleiades.
And that was what the boughs were full of soon.

THE ONSET

Always the same, when on a fated night
At last the gathered snow lets down as white
As may be in dark woods, and with a song
It shall not make again all winter long
Of hissing on the yet uncovered ground,
I almost stumble looking up and round,
As one who overtaken by the end
Gives up his errand, and lets death descend
Upon him where he is, with nothing done
To evil, no important triumph won,
More than if life had never been begun.

Yet all the precedent is on my side:
I know that winter death has never tried
The earth but it has failed: the snow may heap
In long storms an undrifted four feet deep
As measured against maple, birch and oak,
It cannot check the peeper's silver croak;
And I shall see the snow all go down hill
In water of a slender April rill
That flashes tail through last year's withered brake
And dead weeds, like a disappearing snake.
Nothing will be left white but here a birch,
And there a clump of houses with a church.

SPRING POOLS

These pools that, though in forests, still reflect
The total sky almost without defect,
And like the flowers beside them, chill and shiver,
Will like the flowers beside them soon be gone,
And yet not out by any brook or river,
But up by roots to bring dark foliage on.

The trees that have it in their pent-up buds
To darken nature and be summer woods—
Let them think twice before they use their powers
To blot out and drink up and sweep away
These flowery waters and these watery flowers
From snow that melted only yesterday.

IN A DISUSED GRAVEYARD

The living come with grassy tread
To read the gravestones on the hill;
The graveyard draws the living still,
But never any more the dead.

The verses in it say and say:
"The ones who living come today
To read the stones and go away
Tomorrow dead will come to stay."

So sure of death the marbles rhyme,
Yet can't help marking all the time
How no one dead will seem to come.
What is it men are shrinking from?

It would be easy to be clever
And tell the stones: Men hate to die
And have stopped dying now forever.
I think they would believe the lie.

SAND DUNES

Sea waves are green and wet,
But up from where they die,
Rise others vaster yet,
And those are brown and dry.

They are the sea made land
To come at the fisher town,
And bury in solid sand
The men she could not drown.

She may know cove and cape,
But she does not know mankind
If by any change of shape,
She hopes to cut off mind.

Men left her a ship to sink:
They can leave her a hut as well;
And be but more free to think
For the one more cast off shell.

THE BIRTHPLACE

Here further up the mountain slope
Than there was ever any hope,
My father built, enclosed a spring,
Strung chains of wall round everything,
Subdued the growth of earth to grass,
And brought our various lives to pass.
A dozen girls and boys we were.
The mountain seemed to like the stir,
And made of us a little while—
With always something in her smile.
Today she wouldn't know our name.
(No girl's, of course, has stayed the same.)
The mountain pushed us off her knees.
And now her lap is full of trees.

FOR ONCE, THEN, SOMETHING

Others taunt me with having knelt at well-curbs
Always wrong to the light, so never seeing
Deeper down in the well than where the water
Gives me back in a shining surface picture
Me myself in the summer heaven godlike
Looking out of a wreath of fern and cloud puffs.
Once, when trying with chin against a well-curb,
I discerned, as I thought, beyond the picture,
Through the picture, a something white, uncertain,
Something more of the depths—and then I lost it.
Water came to rebuke the too clear water.
One drop fell from a fern, and lo, a ripple
Shook whatever it was lay there at bottom,
Blurred it, blotted it out. What was that whiteness?
Truth? A pebble of quartz? For once, then, something.

A SERIOUS STEP LIGHTLY TAKEN

Between two burrs on the map
Was a hollow-headed snake.
The burrs were hills, the snake was a stream,
And the hollow head was a lake.

And the dot in *front* of a name
Was what should be a town.
And there might be a house we could buy
For only a dollar down.

With two wheels low in the ditch
We left our boiling car,
And knocked at the door of a house we found
And there to-day we are.

It is turning three hundred years
On our cisatlantic shore
For family after family name.
We'll make it three hundred more

For our name farming here,
Aloof yet not aloof,
Enriching soil and increasing stock,
Repairing fence and roof;

A hundred thousand days
Of front-page paper events,
A half a dozen major wars,
And forty-five presidents.

TREE AT MY WINDOW

Tree at my window, window tree,
My sash is lowered when night comes on;
But let there never be curtain drawn
Between you and me.

Vague dream-head lifted out of the ground,
And thing next most diffuse to cloud,
Not all your light tongues talking aloud
Could be profound.

But tree, I have seen you taken and tossed,
And if you have seen me when I slept,
You have seen me when I was taken and swept
And all but lost.

That day she put our heads together,
Fate had her imagination about her,
Your head so much concerned with outer,
Mine with inner, weather.

Although they were first printed in two different books and are not connected in any way, "Sitting by a Bush in Broad Sunlight" and "Stopping by Woods on a Snowy Evening" might be a matching pair of poems. Even the titles supplement each other.

On the surface, both seem to be simple, descriptive verses, records of close observation, graphic and homely pictures. Both use the simplest terms and commonest words: in the two poems there are just four words of three syllables; twenty-nine are two-syllable words; and about two hundred words are words of one syllable. But both poems are deeply meditative; both add far-reaching meanings to the homely music. "Sitting by a Bush in Broad Sunlight" ends on a note of persistent faith. "Stopping by Woods on a Snowy Evening," one of the most quietly moving of Frost's lyrics, uses its superb craftsmanship to come to a climax of responsibility: the promises to be kept, the obligations to be fulfilled. Few poems have said so much in so little.

SITTING BY A BUSH IN BROAD SUNLIGHT

When I spread out my hand here to-day,
I catch no more than a ray
To feel of between thumb and fingers;
No lasting effect of it lingers.

There was one time and only the one
When dust really took in the sun;
And from that one intake of fire
All creatures still warmly suspire.

And if men have watched a long time
And never seen sun-smitten slime
Again come to life and crawl off,
We must not be too ready to scoff.

God once declared he was true
And then took the veil and withdrew,
And remember how final a hush
Then descended of old on the bush.

God once spoke to people by name.
The sun once imparted its flame.
One impulse persists as our breath;
The other persists as our faith.

STOPPING BY WOODS ON A SNOWY EVENING

Whose woods these are I think I know.
His house is in the village though;
He will not see me stopping here
To watch his woods fill up with snow.

My little horse must think it queer
To stop without a farmhouse near
Between the woods and frozen lake
The darkest evening of the year.

He gives his harness bells a shake
To ask if there is some mistake.
The only other sound's the sweep
Of easy wind and downy flake.

The woods are lovely, dark and deep.
But I have promises to keep,
And miles to go before I sleep,
And miles to go before I sleep.

V

THE RUNAWAY AND OTHER ANIMALS

Although Robert Frost is not to be classified as a "nature poet," he knows more about nature than most of his living contemporaries, more even than most of the poets of the past, with the possible exception of Vergil and Wordsworth. Like Coleridge, Frost believes:

> He prayeth best, who loveth best
> All things both great and small.

Frost's love of things "both great and small" includes birds (among which he rates the barnyard hen almost as high as the singing thrush), dogs, woodchucks, cows, and horses. He does not even draw the line at insects. Some of his shrewdest and most delightful—and most sympathetic—poems are about ants and fireflies and spiders and even hornets.

Birds, however, seem to hold the highest place in his affection. Especially characteristic is his tribute to "The Oven Bird," a kind of thrush which builds a nest resembling an oven. This is a bird that voices his knowledge of the changing seasons. And his is the gift of the poet: he knows "what to make of a diminished thing."

THE OVEN BIRD

There is a singer everyone has heard,
Loud, a mid-summer and a mid-wood bird,
Who makes the solid tree trunks sound again.
He says that leaves are old and that for flowers
Mid-summer is to spring as one to ten.
He says the early petal-fall is past
When pear and cherry bloom went down in showers
On sunny days a moment overcast;
And comes that other fall we name the fall.
He says the highway dust is over all.
The bird would cease and be as other birds
But that he knows in singing not to sing.
The question that he frames in all but words
Is what to make of a diminished thing.

.   .   .

"Our Singing Strength" is all in praise of birds. But it is
also a poem in praise of those strugglers and singers who are
not daunted by storms or defeated by adversity:

Well, something for a snowstorm to have shown
The country's singing strength thus brought together,
That though repressed and moody with the weather
Was none the less there ready to be freed
And sing the wildflowers up from root and seed.

Acclaiming its singers great and small, the poet acclaims
America.

OUR SINGING STRENGTH

It snowed in spring on earth so dry and warm
The flakes could find no landing place to form.
Hordes spent themselves to make it wet and cold,
And still they failed of any lasting hold.
They made no white impression on the black.
They disappeared as if earth sent them back.
Not till from separate flakes they changed at night
To almost strips and tapes of ragged white
Did grass and garden ground confess it snowed,
And all go back to winter but the road.
Next day the scene was piled and puffed and dead.
The grass lay flattened under one great tread.
Borne down until the end almost took root,
The rangey bough anticipated fruit
With snowballs cupped in every opening bud.
The road alone maintained itself in mud,
Whatever its secret was of greater heat
From inward fires or brush of passing feet.

In spring more mortal singers than belong
To any one place cover us with song.
Thrush, bluebird, blackbird, sparrow, and robin throng;
Some to go further north to Hudson's Bay,
Some that have come too far north back away,
Really a very few to build and stay.
Now was seen how these liked belated snow.
The fields had nowhere left for them to go;
They'd soon exhausted all there was in flying;
The trees they'd had enough of with once trying

And setting off their heavy powder load.
They could find nothing open but the road.
So there they let their lives be narrowed in
By thousands the bad weather made akin.
The road became a channel running flocks
Of glossy birds like ripples over rocks.
I drove them under foot in bits of flight
That kept the ground, almost disputing right
Of way with me from apathy of wing,
A talking twitter all they had to sing.
A few I must have driven to despair
Made quick asides, but having done in air
A whir among white branches great and small
As in some too much carven marble hall
Where one false wing beat would have brought down all,
Came tamely back in front of me, the Drover,
To suffer the same driven nightmare over.
One such storm in a lifetime couldn't teach them
That back behind pursuit it couldn't reach them;
None flew behind me to be left alone.

Well, something for a snowstorm to have shown
The country's singing strength thus brought together,
That though repressed and moody with the weather
Was none the less there ready to be freed
And sing the wildflowers up from root and seed.

The birds evoked in the three poems which follow are remarkably dissimilar. Some, like the bird in the first poem, sing exasperatingly; some, like the songsters in the second poem, sing enchantingly; some, like the prize creature in the third poem, do not sing at all. All are poems of esteem. And the second is more than a song of praise: a love poem.

A MINOR BIRD

I have wished a bird would fly away,
And not sing by my house all day;

Have clapped my hands at him from the door
When it seemed as if I could bear no more.

The fault must partly have been in me.
The bird was not to blame for his key.

And of course there must be something wrong
In wanting to silence any song.

NEVER AGAIN WOULD BIRDS' SONG BE THE SAME

He would declare and could himself believe
That the birds there in all the garden round
From having heard the daylong voice of Eve
Had added to their own an oversound,
Her tone of meaning but without the words.
Admittedly an eloquence so soft
Could only have had an influence upon birds
When call or laughter carried it aloft.

Be that as may be, she was in their song.
Moreover, her voice upon their voices crossed
Had now persisted in the woods so long
That probably it never would be lost.
Never again would birds' song be the same.

And to do that to birds was why she came.

"A Blue Ribbon at Amesbury" is not only a poet's tribute but a chicken fancier's poem. It is written in deference to the hen which, though handsomely feathered, is not decked out merely for show but might well be the mother of a new and sturdy race; a pullet whose will and shoulders are so strong "she makes the whole flock move along." One wonders why the author (as classicist, humorist, and most of all, as hen-lover) did not write the poem in hendecasyllabics!

As a matter of fact, another poem in this volume *is* written entirely in that classical form. "For Once, Then, Something" (page 189) shows an unusual employment of the hendecasyllabic, that difficult line of eleven metrical syllables.

A BLUE RIBBON AT AMESBURY

Such a fine pullet ought to go
All coiffured to a winter show,
And be exhibited, and win.
The answer is this one has been—

And come with all her honors home.
Her golden leg, her coral comb,
Her fluff of plumage, white as chalk,
Her style, were all the fancy's talk.

It seems as if you must have heard.
She scored an almost perfect bird.
In her we make ourselves acquainted
With one a Sewell might have painted.

Here common with the flock again,
At home in her abiding pen,
She lingers feeding at the trough,
The last to let night drive her off.

The one who gave her ankle-band,
Her keeper, empty pail in hand,
He lingers too, averse to slight
His chores for all the wintry night.

He leans against the dusty wall,
Immured almost beyond recall,
A depth past many swinging doors
And many litter-muffled floors.

He meditates the breeder's art.
He has a half a mind to start,
With her for Mother Eve, a race
That shall all living things displace.

'Tis ritual with her to lay
The full six days, then rest a day;
At which rate barring broodiness
She well may score an egg-success.

The gatherer can always tell
Her well-turned egg's brown sturdy shell,
As safe a vehicle of seed
As is vouchsafed to feathered breed.

No human spectre at the feast
Can scant or hurry her the least.
She takes her time to take her fill.
She whets a sleepy sated bill.

She gropes across the pen alone
To peck herself a precious stone.
She waters at the patent fount.
And so to roost, the last to mount.

The roost is her extent of flight.
Yet once she rises to the height,
She shoulders with a wing so strong
She makes the whole flock move along.

The night is setting in to blow.
It scours the windowpane with snow,

But barely gets from them or her
For comment a complacent chirr.

The lowly pen is yet a hold
Against the dark and wind and cold
To give a prospect to a plan
And warrant prudence in a man.

One of Frost's most graphic poems is about a bird who is
not only unheard but unseen. It seems purely pictorial at
first, but the spirit of the poet adds music as well as meaning
to the silent picture.

LOOKING FOR A SUNSET BIRD IN WINTER

The west was getting out of gold,
The breath of air had died of cold,
When shoeing home across the white,
I thought I saw a bird alight.

In summer when I passed the place
I had to stop and lift my face;
A bird with an angelic gift
Was singing in it sweet and swift.

No bird was singing in it now.
A single leaf was on a bough,

And that was all there was to see
In going twice around the tree.

From my advantage on a hill
I judged that such a crystal chill
Was only adding frost to snow
As gilt to gold that wouldn't show.

A brush had left a crooked stroke
Of what was either cloud or smoke
From north to south across the blue;
A piercing little star was through.

. . .

A drumlin is a ridge or narrow hill made by a glacier
pushing its way through prehistoric land. It forms a fine re-
treat, the very sort of rocky burrow favored by the wood-
chuck, or ground hog.

In a set of half-humorous, half-symbolic lines the poet
identifies himself with the shrewd woodchuck: an animal
which, unlike the beaver, has nothing to do with wood, but
is so called because that is the way the pioneers heard the
original American Indian name "wejack."

A DRUMLIN WOODCHUCK

One thing has a shelving bank,
Another a rotting plank,
To give it cozier skies
And make up for its lack of size.

My own strategic retreat
Is where two rocks almost meet,

And still more secure and snug,
A two-door burrow I dug.

With those in mind at my back
I can sit forth exposed to attack
As one who shrewdly pretends
That he and the world are friends.

All we who prefer to live
Have a little whistle we give,
And flash, at the least alarm
We dive down under the farm.

We allow some time for guile
And don't come out for a while
Either to eat or drink.
We take occasion to think.

And if after the hunt goes past
And the double-barrelled blast
(Like war and pestilence
And the loss of common sense),

If I can with confidence say
That still for another day,
Or even another year,
I will be there for you, my dear,

It will be because, though small
As measured against the All,
I have been so instinctively thorough
About my crevice and burrow.

This poet knows animals as well as he knows people. Perhaps he inherited that knowledge. Perhaps it is more than a coincidence that the "strange device" of the Lincolnshire Frosts, from whom the poet is descended, is an emblem showing a pine tree topped by a triumphant squirrel.

Frost's poems about insects are broadly humorous. If, as the Psalms tell us, man was made "a little lower than the angels," Frost implies that insects, for all their apparent skill, are a little lower than animals and considerably lower than man. In "The White-tailed Hornet" he pokes fun at the theory that "to err is human" but that insects never make mistakes. His droll and unblinking account of the blundering hornet is a point against those who rely on the "infallibility of instinct."

THE WHITE-TAILED HORNET

The white-tailed hornet lives in a balloon
That floats against the ceiling of the woodshed.
The exit he comes out at like a bullet
Is like the pupil of a pointed gun.
And having power to change his aim in flight,
He comes out more unerring than a bullet.
Verse could be written on the certainty
With which he penetrates my best defense
Of whirling hands and arms about the head
To stab me in the sneeze-nerve of a nostril.
Such is the instinct of it I allow.
Yet how about the insect certainty
That in the neighborhood of home and children
Is such an execrable judge of motives
As not to recognize in me the exception
I like to think I am in everything—
One who would never hang above a bookcase
His Japanese crepe-paper globe for trophy?
He stung me first and stung me afterward.
He rolled me off the field head over heels,
And would not listen to my explanations.

That's when I went as visitor to his house.
As visitor at my house he is better.
Hawking for flies about the kitchen door,
In at one door perhaps and out another,
Trust him then not to put you in the wrong.
He won't misunderstand your freest movements.
Let him light on your skin unless you mind
So many prickly grappling feet at once.

He's after the domesticated fly
To feed his thumping grubs as big as he is.
Here he is at his best, but even here—
I watched him where he swooped, he pounced, he struck;
But what he found he had was just a nailhead.
He struck a second time. Another nailhead.
"Those are just nailheads. Those are fastened down."
Then disconcerted and not unannoyed,
He stooped and struck a little huckleberry
The way a player curls around a football.
"Wrong shape, wrong color, and wrong scent," I said.
The huckleberry rolled him on his head.
At last it was a fly. He shot and missed;
And the fly circled round him in derision.
But for the fly he might have made me think
He had been at his poetry, comparing
Nailhead with fly and fly with huckleberry:
How like a fly, how very like a fly.
But the real fly he missed would never do;
The missed fly made me dangerously skeptic.

Won't this whole instinct matter bear revision?
Won't almost any theory bear revision?
To err is human, not to, animal.
Or so we pay the compliment to instinct,
Only too liberal of our compliment
That really takes away instead of gives.
Our worship, humor, conscientiousness
Went long since to the dogs under the table.
And served us right for having instituted
Downward comparisons. As long on earth
As our comparisons were stoutly upward
With gods and angels, we were men at least,

But little lower than the gods and angels.
But once comparisons were yielded downward,
Once we began to see our images
Reflected in the mud and even dust,
'Twas disillusion upon disillusion.
We were lost piecemeal to the animals,
Like people thrown out to delay the wolves.
Nothing but fallibility was left us,
And this day's work made even that seem doubtful.

WASPISH

On glossy wires artistically bent,
He draws himself up to his full extent.
His natty wings with self-assurance perk.
His stinging quarters menacingly work.
Poor egotist, he has no way of knowing
But he's as good as anybody going.

.   .   .

"Departmental" is one of the most frankly comic of
Frost's poems. As originally printed, there was a subtitle that
contained a pun: "The End of My Ant Jerry." The high
humor was (and still is) emphasized by the comic rhymes,
especially the rhymes for "Jerry" and "Formic," the latter
proving that the poor victim was a house ant, *Formica*.

But, though the lines provoke laughter, the poem is much
more than a set of burlesque verses. Before the reader is
halfway through, he is aware that "Departmental" is a
satire, a criticism of standardization. The irony of regimen-
tation is wryly pronounced by the rueful end.

DEPARTMENTAL

An ant on the table cloth
Ran into a dormant moth
Of many times his size.
He showed not the least surprise.
His business wasn't with such.
He gave it scarcely a touch,
And was off on his duty run.
Yet if he encountered one
Of the hive's enquiry squad
Whose work is to find out God
And the nature of time and space,
He would put him onto the case.
Ants are a curious race;
One crossing with hurried tread
The body of one of their dead
Isn't given a moment's arrest—
Seems not even impressed.
But he no doubt reports to any
With whom he crosses antennae,
And they no doubt report
To the higher up at court.
Then word goes forth in Formic:
"Death's come to Jerry McCormic,
Our selfless forager Jerry.
Will the special Janizary
Whose office it is to bury
The dead of the commissary
Go bring him home to his people.

Lay him in state on a sepal.
Wrap him for shroud in a petal.
Embalm him with ichor of nettle.
This is the word of your Queen."
And presently on the scene
Appears a solemn mortician;
And taking formal position
With feelers calmly atwiddle,
Seizes the dead by the middle,
And heaving him high in air,
Carries him out of there.
No one stands round to stare.
It is nobody else's affair.

It couldn't be called ungentle.
But how thoroughly departmental.

·   ·   ·

The poet has a special sympathy for the persistent firefly and the patient spider. He does not laugh at the "emulating flies" who try to imitate stars, even though "they can't sustain the part."

The "heal-all" is a common country plant supposed to have healing properties; it is almost always blue in color. The poet has found a strange white variety and, stranger still, attached to it a white spinner, "a snow-drop spider," holding a white moth, completing a pattern of whiteness. Here, in a world of chaos and darkness, there is purpose and design—"if" (the poet speculates whimsically) "design govern in a thing so small."

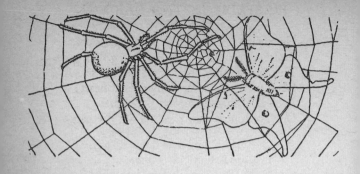

DESIGN

I found a dimpled spider, fat and white,
On a white heal-all, holding up a moth
Like a white piece of rigid satin cloth—
Assorted characters of death and blight
Mixed ready to begin the morning right,
Like the ingredients of a witches' broth—
A snow-drop spider, a flower like froth,
And dead wings carried like a paper kite.

What had that flower to do with being white,
The wayside blue and innocent heal-all?
What brought the kindred spider to that height,
Then steered the white moth thither in the night?
What but design of darkness to appall?—
If design govern in a thing so small.

Here come real stars to fill the upper skies,
And here on earth come emulating flies,
That though they never equal stars in size,
(And they were never really stars at heart)
Achieve at times a very star-like start.
Only, of course, they can't sustain the part.

·   ·   ·

"Canis Major" is a dog poem in several senses. The title
indicates it is primarily about the Great Dog, that constella-
tion which includes Sirius, the dog star, "in one eye." But
the poem also concerns the underdog, even though the poet
barely touches upon this earthly and oppressed creature.

CANIS MAJOR

The great Overdog,
That heavenly beast
With a star in one eye,
Gives a leap in the east.

He dances upright
All the way to the west
And never once drops
On his forefeet to rest.

I'm a poor underdog,
But tonight I will bark
With the great Overdog
That romps through the dark.

"Two Look at Two" is a tribute in which emotion is beautifully expressed without being exploited, a love poem in which the word "love" is mentioned only twice, literally as the first word and the last word.

It is also a poem in which the animals and the human beings are subtly paired. As James Southall Wilson wrote in an appreciation entitled "In Human Terms": "When the two lovers come face to face with the buck and his doe, it is human nature facing deer nature. Such a picture might be symbolical of how nature and man reflect each other in Frost's poetry." But it is the emotion which rises like "a great wave" from the poem, and which remains, burning in the air, after the poem is over.

> As if the earth in one unlooked-for favor
> Had made them certain earth returned their love.

TWO LOOK AT TWO

Love and forgetting might have carried them
A little further up the mountain side
With night so near, but not much further up.
They must have halted soon in any case
With thoughts of the path back, how rough it was
With rock and washout, and unsafe in darkness;
When they were halted by a tumbled wall
With barbed-wire binding. They stood facing this,
Spending what onward impulse they still had
In one last look the way they must not go,

On up the failing path, where, if a stone
Or earthslide moved at night, it moved itself;
No footstep moved it. "This is all," they sighed,
"Good-night to woods." But not so; there was more.
A doe from round a spruce stood looking at them
Across the wall, as near the wall as they.
She saw them in their field, they her in hers.
The difficulty of seeing what stood still,
Like some up-ended boulder split in two,
Was in her clouded eyes: they saw no fear there.
She seemed to think that two thus they were safe.
Then, as if they were something that, though strange,
She could not trouble her mind with too long,
She sighed and passed unscared along the wall.
"*This,* then, is all. What more is there to ask?"
But no, not yet. A snort to bid them wait.
A buck from round the spruce stood looking at them
Across the wall as near the wall as they.
This was an antlered buck of lusty nostril,
Not the same doe come back into her place.
He viewed them quizzically with jerks of head,
As if to ask, "Why don't you make some motion?
Or give some sign of life? Because you can't.
I doubt if you're as living as you look."
Thus till he had them almost feeling dared
To stretch a proffering hand—and a spell-breaking.
Then he too passed unscared along the wall.
Two had seen two, whichever side you spoke from.
"This *must* be all." It was all. Still they stood,
A great wave from it going over them,
As if the earth in one unlooked-for favor
Had made them certain earth returned their love.

"The Cow in Apple Time" is a simple pastoral and frankly humorous picture. Yet some commentators have read astonishing things into it. One critic has said the cow was "mad," although it was not specified whether the poor beast was mad with rage or with insanity. Another commentator saw in the cow a symbol of determination, and in her cavortings a demonstration of "her superiority to mankind bent on confining her."

The true reason for the cow's unreasonably high spirits is implied in the title. This cow has eaten too many ripe apples and, as a result, "scorns a pasture withering to the root." Drunk with cider, her face "flecked with pomace," she leaps over gates and walls and any other barriers that stand in the way of her tipsy carouse.

THE COW IN APPLE TIME

Something inspires the only cow of late
To make no more of a wall than an open gate,
And think no more of wall-builders than fools.
Her face is flecked with pomace and she drools
A cider syrup. Having tasted fruit,
She scorns a pasture withering to the root.
She runs from tree to tree where lie and sweeten
The windfalls spiked with stubble and worm-eaten.
She leaves them bitten when she has to fly.
She bellows on a knoll against the sky.
Her udder shrivels and the milk goes dry.

More reckless if less restricted than "The Cow in Apple Time," the unsteady progress of the bear is not as carefree as it may seem. Frost regards the bear not as a creature of footloose freedom, but as a symbol of mortal perplexity. Here is a satirical comparison of the uncaged bear and man trapped in the endless conflict between mind and mood. Here the human animal, looking hopefully toward science, longing for logic, but still leaning heavily on instinct, is caught midway between reason and emotion—a spectacle no less comic for being equally pathetic.

The lines follow the unhappy progress with careful delicacy; beginning with gentle humor, the poem ends with mocking wit.

THE BEAR

The bear puts both arms around the tree above her
And draws it down as if it were a lover
And its choke cherries lips to kiss good-bye,
Then lets it snap back upright in the sky.
Her next step rocks a boulder on the wall
(She's making her cross-country in the fall).
Her great weight creaks the barbed-wire in its staples
As she flings over and off down through the maples,
Leaving on one wire tooth a lock of hair.
Such is the uncaged progress of the bear.
The world has room to make a bear feel free;

The universe seems cramped to you and me.
Man acts more like the poor bear in a cage
That all day fights a nervous inward rage,
His mood rejecting all his mind suggests.
He paces back and forth and never rests
The toe-nail click and shuffle of his feet,
The telescope at one end of his beat,
And at the other end the microscope,
Two instruments of nearly equal hope,
And in conjunction giving quite a spread.
Or if he rests from scientific tread,
'Tis only to sit back and sway his head
Through ninety odd degrees of arc, it seems,
Between two metaphysical extremes.
He sits back on his fundamental butt
With lifted snout and eyes (if any) shut,
(He almost looks religious but he's not),
And back and forth he sways from cheek to cheek,
At one extreme agreeing with one Greek,
At the other agreeing with another Greek
Which may be thought, but only so to speak.
A baggy figure, equally pathetic
When sedentary and when peripatetic.

"The Runaway" tells something which, it seems, might have been observed anywhere; yet a few hints establish the scene as definitely local. The name Morgan tells the reader that this is an American horse, a horse bred in Vermont, only a few miles from the poet's farm near Bread Loaf Mountain. The accent, too, is American:

> I doubt if even his mother could tell him, "Sakes,
> It's only weather!"

American also is the quiet hint of early snow, of frost that strikes New England fields sometimes as early as August. Startled, the little animal which has never seen snow "shudders his coat," as if to get rid of these white and coldly stinging flies. An outspoken tenderness depicts astonishment in the colt's "whited eyes," and a threatening heaven is suggested in "the miniature thunder" of his scampering hoofs.

THE RUNAWAY

Once when the snow of the year was beginning to fall,
We stopped by a mountain pasture to say, "Whose colt?"
A little Morgan had one forefoot on the wall,
The other curled at his breast. He dipped his head
And snorted at us. And then he had to bolt.
We heard the miniature thunder where he fled,
And we saw him, or thought we saw him, dim and grey
Like a shadow against the curtain of falling flakes.
"I think the little fellow's afraid of the snow.
He isn't winter-broken. It isn't play
With the little fellow at all. He's running away.
I doubt if even his mother could tell him, 'Sakes,
It's only weather.' He'd think she didn't know!
Where is his mother? He can't be out alone."
And now he comes again with clatter of stone,
And mounts the wall again with whited eyes
And all his tail that isn't hair up straight.
He shudders his coat as if to throw off flies.
"Whoever it is that leaves him out so late,
When other creatures have gone to stall and bin,
Ought to be told to come and take him in."

VI

COUNTRY THINGS AND OTHER THINGS

Robert Frost has gone his own way. He could not help it; his destination—and perhaps his destiny—was directed by the spirit behind the man. This inevitable progress is indicated in a much-quoted and much-misunderstood poem, "The Road Not Taken." Once while traveling alone, Frost tells us, he stood at a fork in the road, undecided which path to take. Finally, he chose one because it seemed a little less frequented, though actually there was no such difference, for "the passing there had worn them really about the same." Yet, even at the moment of choice, the poet quizzically imagined that the choice was important, that he would someday tell himself he took the less traveled road:

And that has made all the difference.

The poet's "difference" is in him from the beginning, long before he sets out on his career. The road that Robert Frost took was not only the "different" road, the right road for him, but the only road he could have taken.

THE ROAD NOT TAKEN

Two roads diverged in a yellow wood,
And sorry I could not travel both
And be one traveler, long I stood
And looked down one as far as I could
To where it bent in the undergrowth;

Then took the other, as just as fair,
And having perhaps the better claim,
Because it was grassy and wanted wear;
Though as for that the passing there
Had worn them really about the same,

And both that morning equally lay
In leaves no step had trodden black.
Oh, I kept the first for another day!
Yet knowing how way leads on to way,
I doubted if I should ever come back.

I shall be telling this with a sigh
Somewhere ages and ages hence:
Two roads diverged in a wood, and I—
I took the one less traveled by,
And that has made all the difference.

A living poem is one that stays alive because it is rooted in mortal things and deathless emotions. It is felt first and thought out afterwards. "It begins," Frost once wrote in a letter, "with a lump in the throat, a homesickness or a love-sickness. It is a reaching-out toward expression; an effort to find fulfillment. A complete poem is one where an emotion has found its thought, and the thought has found the words."

Frost's lyrics, more personal than poems about people and events, take the reader with suddenness and surprise. Here, with immediate appeal, "emotion has found its thought, and the thought has found the words." Frost, more than most, is versed not only in "country things," but in things beyond scrutiny, beyond even the sharpest examination. In the poet's world, vision has been added to observation, and the power of sight has been strengthened by insight.

THE NEED OF BEING VERSED IN COUNTRY
THINGS

The house had gone to bring again
To the midnight sky a sunset glow.
Now the chimney was all of the house that stood,
Like a pistil after the petals go.

The barn opposed across the way,
That would have joined the house in flame
Had it been the will of the wind, was left
To bear forsaken the place's name.

No more it opened with all one end
For teams that came by the stony road
To drum on the floor with scurrying hoofs
And brush the mow with the summer load.

The birds that came to it through the air
At broken windows flew out and in,
Their murmur more like the sigh we sigh
From too much dwelling on what has been.

Yet for them the lilac renewed its leaf,
And the aged elm, though touched with fire;
And the dry pump flung up an awkward arm;
And the fence post carried a strand of wire.

For them there was really nothing sad.
But though they rejoiced in the nest they kept,
One had to be versed in country things
Not to believe the phoebes wept.

THE SOUND OF THE TREES

I wonder about the trees.
Why do we wish to bear
Forever the noise of these
More than another noise
So close to our dwelling place?
We suffer them by the day
Till we lose all measure of pace,
And fixity in our joys,
And acquire a listening air.
They are that that talks of going
But never gets away;
And that talks no less for knowing,
As it grows wiser and older,
That now it means to stay.
My feet tug at the floor
And my head sways to my shoulder
Sometimes when I watch trees sway,
From the window or the door.
I shall set forth for somewhere,
I shall make the reckless choice
Some day when they are in voice
And tossing so as to scare
The white clouds over them on.
I shall have less to say,
But I shall be gone.

IN HARDWOOD GROVES

The same leaves over and over again!
They fall from giving shade above
To make one texture of faded brown
And fit the earth like a leather glove.

Before the leaves can mount again
To fill the trees with another shade,
They must go down past things coming up,
They must go down into the dark decayed.

They *must* be pierced by flowers and put
Beneath the feet of dancing flowers.
However it is in some other world
I know that this is the way in ours.

NOTHING GOLD CAN STAY

Nature's first green is gold,
Her hardest hue to hold.
Her early leaf's a flower;
But only so an hour.
Then leaf subsides to leaf.
So Eden sank to grief,
So dawn goes down to day.
Nothing gold can stay.

"After Apple-Picking" is so vivid a memory of experience that the reader absorbs it physically. He smells the heady scent of apples; senses the strangeness of the world as it seems to the overtired worker; feels how definitely the instep arch

> . . . not only keeps the ache,
> It keeps the pressure of a ladder-round.

It is all so simple and exact, so casual yet so original. A poem of reality, "After Apple-Picking" has the enchantment of a lingering dream.

AFTER APPLE-PICKING

My long two-pointed ladder's sticking through a tree
Toward heaven still,
And there's a barrel that I didn't fill
Beside it, and there may be two or three
Apples I didn't pick upon some bough.
But I am done with apple-picking now.
Essence of winter sleep is on the night,
The scent of apples: I am drowsing off.
I cannot rub the strangeness from my sight
I got from looking through a pane of glass

I skimmed this morning from the drinking trough
And held against the world of hoary grass.
It melted, and I let it fall and break.
But I was well
Upon my way to sleep before it fell,
And I could tell
What form my dreaming was about to take.
Magnified apples appear and disappear,
Stem end and blossom end,
And every fleck of russet showing clear.
My instep arch not only keeps the ache,
It keeps the pressure of a ladder-round.
I feel the ladder sway as the boughs bend.
And I keep hearing from the cellar bin
The rumbling sound
Of load on load of apples coming in.
For I have had too much
Of apple-picking: I am overtired
Of the great harvest I myself desired.
There were ten thousand thousand fruit to touch,
Cherish in hand, lift down, and not let fall.
For all
That struck the earth,
No matter if not bruised or spiked with stubble,
Went surely to the cider-apple heap
As of no worth.
One can see what will trouble
This sleep of mine, whatever sleep it is.
Were he not gone,
The woodchuck could say whether it's like his
Long sleep, as I describe its coming on,
Or just some human sleep.

Frost's devotion to fact shines particularly through his shorter poems. But his is never a mere transcript of actuality, a kind of dogged reporting. When he is most faithful to *things*, he is most lyrical. "The Grindstone" is a familiar portrait, a still-life painting of the tool-sharpening instrument common to every farmyard. Yet a whimsical fantasy takes possession with the opening lines:

> Having a wheel and four legs of its own
> Has never availed the cumbersome grindstone
> To get it anywhere that I can see.

As the poem gathers speed, it accumulates wit and inventiveness. The grindstone turns in an acceleration of energy, and, after achieving its highest momentum, it suddenly slows down—slows down, as it were, from fantasy to philosophy.

THE GRINDSTONE

Having a wheel and four legs of its own
Has never availed the cumbersome grindstone
To get it anywhere that I can see.
These hands have helped it go, and even race;
Not all the motion, though, they ever lent,
Not all the miles it may have thought it went,
Have got it one step from the starting place.
It stands beside the same old apple tree.
The shadow of the apple tree is thin
Upon it now, its feet are fast in snow.
All other farm machinery's gone in,
And some of it on no more legs and wheel
Than the grindstone can boast to stand or go.
(I'm thinking chiefly of the wheelbarrow.)
For months it hasn't known the taste of steel,

Washed down with rusty water in a tin.
But standing outdoors hungry, in the cold,
Except in towns at night, is not a sin.
And, anyway, its standing in the yard
Under a ruinous live apple tree
Has nothing any more to do with me,
Except that I remember how of old
One summer day, all day I drove it hard,
And someone mounted on it rode it hard,
And he and I between us ground a blade.

I gave it the preliminary spin,
And poured on water (tears it might have been);
And when it almost gayly jumped and flowed,
A Father-Time-like man got on and rode,
Armed with a scythe and spectacles that glowed.
He turned on will-power to increase the load
And slow me down—and I abruptly slowed,
Like coming to a sudden railroad station.
I changed from hand to hand in desperation.
I wondered what machine of ages gone
This represented an improvement on.
For all I knew it may have sharpened spears
And arrowheads itself. Much use for years
Had gradually worn it an oblate
Spheroid that kicked and struggled in its gait,
Appearing to return me hate for hate
(But I forgive it now as easily
As any other boyhood enemy
Whose pride has failed to get him anywhere).
I wondered who it was the man thought ground—
The one who held the wheel back or the one
Who gave his life to keep it going round?

I wondered if he really thought it fair
For him to have the say when we were done.
Such were the bitter thoughts to which I turned.

Not for myself was I so much concerned.
Oh no!—although, of course, I could have found
A better way to pass the afternoon
Than grinding discord out of a grindstone,
And beating insects at their gritty tune.
Nor was I for the man so much concerned.
Once when the grindstone almost jumped its bearing
It looked as if he might be badly thrown
And wounded on his blade. So far from caring,
I laughed inside, and only cranked the faster
(It ran as if it wasn't greased but glued);
I'd welcome any moderate disaster
That might be calculated to postpone
What evidently nothing could conclude.
The thing that made me more and more afraid
Was that we'd ground it sharp and hadn't known,
And now were only wasting precious blade.
And when he raised it dripping once and tried
The creepy edge of it with wary touch,
And viewed it over his glasses funny-eyed,
Only disinterestedly to decide
It needed a turn more, I could have cried.
Wasn't there danger of a turn too much?
Mightn't we make it worse instead of better?
I was for leaving something to the whetter.
What if it wasn't all it should be? I'd
Be satisfied if he'd be satisfied.

Fact and fancy are beautifully balanced in the lyrics. Nothing escapes the poet's observation; nothing prevents his speculation upon what he observes. He sees how, in order to save a little time and material, some masons build a chimney beginning halfway up the wall "on a shelf." But the poet will have none of this. He wants his chimney "clear from the ground." At first he gives good, even matter-of-fact, reasons for this. But at the end he confesses that he does not want to deceive himself with illusions. He wants his chimney planted in the earth because he does not want to be reminded of castles he used to build in the air.

THE KITCHEN CHIMNEY

Builder, in building the little house,
In every way you may please yourself;
But please please me in the kitchen chimney:
Don't build me a chimney upon a shelf.

However far you must go for bricks,
Whatever they cost a-piece or a pound,
Buy me enough for a full-length chimney,
And build the chimney clear from the ground.

It's not that I'm greatly afraid of fire,
But I never heard of a house that throve
(And I know of one that didn't thrive)
Where the chimney started above the stove.

And I dread the ominous stain of tar
That there always is on the papered walls,

And the smell of fire drowned in rain
That there always is when the chimney's false.

A shelf's for a clock or vase or picture,
But I don't see why it should have to bear
A chimney that only would serve to remind me
Of castles I used to build in air.

Observation and imagination, experience and intuition, mingle unforgettably in Frost's lyrics. They add excitement to such a humble task as gathering leaves; they illuminate such common sights as a hillside thaw, a tree fallen across the road, a passing glimpse of unrecognized flowers, and a few flakes of powdery snow.

GATHERING LEAVES

Spades take up leaves
No better than spoons,
And bags full of leaves
Are light as balloons.

I make a great noise
Of rustling all day
Like rabbit and deer
Running away.

But the mountains I raise
Elude my embrace,
Flowing over my arms
And into my face.

I may load and unload
Again and again
Till I fill the whole shed,
And what have I then?

Next to nothing for weight;
And since they grew duller
From contact with earth,
Next to nothing for color.

Next to nothing for use.
But a crop is a crop,
And who's to say where
The harvest shall stop?

A LEAF TREADER

I have been treading on leaves all day until I am autumn-
tired.
God knows all the color and form of leaves I have trodden
on and mired.
Perhaps I have put forth too much strength and been too
fierce from fear.
I have safely trodden underfoot the leaves of another year.

All summer long they were over head, more lifted up
than I.
To come to their final place in earth they had to pass me by.
All summer long I thought I heard them threatening under
their breath.
And when they came it seemed with a will to carry me with
them to death.

They spoke to the fugitive in my heart as if it were leaf
to leaf.
They tapped at my eyelids and touched my lips with an
invitation to grief.
But it was no reason I had to go because they had to go.
Now up my knee to keep on top of another year of snow.

A HILLSIDE THAW

To think to know the country and not know
The hillside on the day the sun lets go
Ten million silver lizards out of snow!
As often as I've seen it done before
I can't pretend to tell the way it's done.
It looks as if some magic of the sun
Lifted the rug that bred them on the floor
And the light breaking on them made them run.
But if I thought to stop the wet stampede,
And caught one silver lizard by the tail,
And put my foot on one without avail,
And threw myself wet-elbowed and wet-kneed
In front of twenty others' wriggling speed,—
In the confusion of them all aglitter,
And birds that joined in the excited fun
By doubling and redoubling song and twitter,
I have no doubt I'd end by holding none.

It takes the moon for this. The sun's a wizard
By all I tell; but so's the moon a witch.
From the high west she makes a gentle cast
And suddenly, without a jerk or twitch,
She has her spell on every single lizard.
I fancied when I looked at six o'clock
The swarm still ran and scuttled just as fast.
The moon was waiting for her chill effect.
I looked at nine: the swarm was turned to rock
In every lifelike posture of the swarm,

Transfixed on mountain slopes almost erect.
Across each other and side by side they lay.
The spell that so could hold them as they were
Was wrought through trees without a breath of storm
To make a leaf, if there had been one, stir.
It was the moon's: she held them until day,
One lizard at the end of every ray.
The thought of my attempting such a stay!

ON A TREE FALLEN ACROSS THE ROAD

(TO HEAR US TALK)

The tree the tempest with a crash of wood
Throws down in front of us is not to bar
Our passage to our journey's end for good,
But just to ask us who we think we are

Insisting always on our own way so.
She likes to halt us in our runner tracks,
And make us get down in a foot of snow
Debating what to do without an axe.

And yet she knows obstruction is in vain:
We will not be put off the final goal
We have it hidden in us to attain,
Not though we have to seize earth by the pole

And, tired of aimless circling in one place,
Steer straight off after something into space.

A PASSING GLIMPSE

TO RIDGELY TORRENCE
ON LAST LOOKING INTO HIS "HESPERIDES"

I often see flowers from a passing car
That are gone before I can tell what they are.

I want to get out of the train and go back
To see what they were beside the track.

I name all the flowers I am sure they weren't:
Not fireweed loving where woods have burnt—

Not blue bells gracing a tunnel mouth—
Not lupine living on sand and drouth.

Was something brushed across my mind
That no one on earth will ever find?

Heaven gives its glimpses only to those
Not in position to look too close.

DUST OF SNOW

The way a crow
Shook down on me
The dust of snow
From a hemlock tree

Has given my heart
A change of mood
And saved some part
Of a day I had rued.

Frost's lyrics range from the facetious to the philosophic; often the two extremes are combined. Mostly, however, they begin with a simple idea and coax the reader, almost without his awareness, to extend the implication of the idea far beyond its plain presentation.

For example, the poet begins a poem entitled "Riders" with the mere notion of riding. But, before the lines have run their course, the reader is led to consider that man is an endlessly adventurous creature and that he may someday mount himself upon the farthest star, for

We have ideas yet that we haven't tried.

To take another example, the abstract idea of speed (in "The Master Speed") conducts the reader, and also the lover, in "a stream of radiance to the sky" and "back through history up the stream of time." More than that, by a quiet paradox it persuades him that he has "the power of standing still." Thus speed and love are joined, and

Two such as you with such a master speed
Cannot be parted nor be swept away. . . .

The union of love and speed may be unusual, but it is no more remarkable than fire and ice. The poem "Fire and Ice" is a masterpiece of condensation. Here, wrapped in an epigram, is a speculation concerning the end of the world and the beginning of wisdom:

FIRE AND ICE

Some say the world will end in fire,
Some say in ice.
From what I've tasted of desire
I hold with those who favor fire.
But if it had to perish twice,
I think I know enough of hate
To say that for destruction ice
Is also great
And would suffice.

RIDERS

The surest thing there is is we are riders,
And though none too successful at it, guiders,
Through everything presented, land and tide
And now the very air, of what we ride.

What is this talked-of mystery of birth
But being mounted bareback on the earth?
We can just see the infant up astride,
His small fist buried in the bushy hide.

There is our wildest mount—a headless horse.
But though it runs unbridled off its course,
And all our blandishments would seem defied,
We have ideas yet that we haven't tried.

THE MASTER SPEED

No speed of wind or water rushing by
But you have speed far greater. You can climb
Back up a stream of radiance to the sky,
And back through history up the stream of time.
And you were given this swiftness, not for haste,
Nor chiefly that you may go where you will,
But in the rush of everything to waste,
That you may have the power of standing still—
Off any still or moving thing you say.
Two such as you with such a master speed
Cannot be parted nor be swept away
From one another once you are agreed
That life is only life forevermore
Together wing to wing and oar to oar.

A Boy's Will, Robert Frost's first book, is chiefly lyrical—the spontaneous upwelling of the youthful heart—but the years have not spoiled its freshness. Such poems as "My November Guest," "Storm Fear," "October," and "Wind and Window Flower" (all from *A Boy's Will*) do not date. They range from a contemplation of the sad beauty of bare autumn to young fancies about an indoor flower wooed by a wintry breeze, yet they are unmistakably the work of the same unaging poet.

MY NOVEMBER GUEST

My Sorrow, when she's here with me,
   Thinks these dark days of autumn rain
Are beautiful as days can be;
She loves the bare, the withered tree;
   She walks the sodden pasture lane.

Her pleasure will not let me stay.
   She talks and I am fain to list:
She's glad the birds are gone away,
She's glad her simple worsted grey
   Is silver now with clinging mist.

The desolate, deserted trees,
   The faded earth, the heavy sky,
The beauties she so truly sees,
She thinks I have no eye for these,
   And vexes me for reason why.

Not yesterday I learned to know
    The love of bare November days
Before the coming of the snow,
But it were vain to tell her so,
    And they are better for her praise.

STORM FEAR

When the wind works against us in the dark,
And pelts with snow
The lower chamber window on the east,
And whispers with a sort of stifled bark,
The beast,
"Come out! Come out!"—
It costs no inward struggle not to go,
Ah, no!
I count our strength,
Two and a child,
Those of us not asleep subdued to mark
How the cold creeps as the fire dies at length,—
How drifts are piled,
Dooryard and road ungraded,
Till even the comforting barn grows far away,
And my heart owns a doubt
Whether 'tis in us to arise with day
And save ourselves unaided.

WIND AND WINDOW FLOWER

Lovers, forget your love,
    And list to the love of these.
She a window flower,
    And he a winter breeze.

When the frosty window veil
    Was melted down at noon,
And the cagèd yellow bird
    Hung over her in tune,

He marked her through the pane
    He could not help but mark,
And only passed her by,
    To come again at dark.

He was a winter wind,
    Concerned with ice and snow,
Dead weeds and unmated birds,
    And little of love could know.

But he sighed upon the sill,
    He gave the sash a shake,
As witness all within
    Who lay that night awake.

Perchance he half prevailed
    To win her for the flight
From the firelit looking-glass
    And warm stove-window light.

But the flower leaned aside
    And thought of naught to say,
And morning found the breeze
    A hundred miles away.

OCTOBER

O hushed October morning mild,
Thy leaves have ripened to the fall;
To-morrow's wind, if it be wild,
Should waste them all.
The crows above the forest call;
To-morrow they may form and go.
O hushed October morning mild,
Begin the hours of this day slow.
Make the day seem to us less brief.
Hearts not averse to being beguiled,
Beguile us in the way you know.
Release one leaf at break of day;
At noon release another leaf;
One from our trees, one far away.
Retard the sun with gentle mist;
Enchant the land with amethyst.
Slow, slow!
For the grapes' sake, if they were all,
Whose leaves already are burnt with frost,
Whose clustered fruit must else be lost—
For the grapes' sake along the wall.

As Frost grew older, his poems grew in range as well as richness. They are sometimes as quizzical as "Good Hours," as naturally fanciful (or as fancifully natural) as "Pea Brush," as mystical and severe as "I Will Sing You One-O," as intensely passionate as "To Earthward." Varied as they are, all bear the signature of the poet, the seal of his personality and the proof of his devotion.

GOOD HOURS

I had for my winter evening walk—
No one at all with whom to talk,
But I had the cottages in a row
Up to their shining eyes in snow.

And I thought I had the folk within:
I had the sound of a violin;
I had a glimpse through curtain laces
Of youthful forms and youthful faces.

I had such company outward bound.
I went till there were no cottages found.
I turned and repented, but coming back
I saw no window but that was black.

Over the snow my creaking feet
Disturbed the slumbering village street
Like profanation, by your leave,
At ten o'clock of a winter eve.

PEA BRUSH

I walked down alone Sunday after church
   To the place where John has been cutting trees
To see for myself about the birch
   He said I could have to bush my peas.

The sun in the new-cut narrow gap
   Was hot enough for the first of May,
And stifling hot with the odor of sap
   From stumps still bleeding their life away.

The frogs that were peeping a thousand shrill
   Wherever the ground was low and wet,
The minute they heard my step went still
   To watch me and see what I came to get.

Birch boughs enough piled everywhere!—
   All fresh and sound from the recent axe.
Time someone came with cart and pair
   And got them off the wild flowers' backs.

They might be good for garden things
   To curl a little finger round,
The same as you seize cat's-cradle strings,
   And lift themselves up off the ground.

Small good to anything growing wild,
   They were crooking many a trillium
That had budded before the boughs were piled
   And since it was coming up had to come.

I WILL SING YOU ONE-O

It was long I lay
Awake that night
Wishing the tower
Would name the hour
And tell me whether
To call it day
(Though not yet light)
And give up sleep.
The snow fell deep
With the hiss of spray;
Two winds would meet,
One down one street,
One down another,
And fight in a smother
Of dust and feather.
I could not say,
But feared the cold
Had checked the pace
Of the tower clock
By tying together
Its hands of gold
Before its face.

Then came one knock!
A note unruffled
Of earthly weather,
Though strange and muffled.
The tower said, "One!"
And then a steeple.

They spoke to themselves
And such few people
As winds might rouse
From sleeping warm
(But not unhouse).
They left the storm
That struck *en masse*
My window glass
Like a beaded fur.
In that grave One
They spoke of the sun
And moon and stars,
Saturn and Mars
And Jupiter.
Still more unfettered,
They left the named
And spoke of the lettered,
The sigmas and taus
Of constellations.
They filled their throats
With the furthest bodies
To which man sends his
Speculation,
Beyond which God is;
The cosmic motes
Of yawning lenses.
Their solemn peals
Were not their own:
They spoke for the clock
With whose vast wheels
Theirs interlock.
In that grave word
Uttered alone

The utmost star
Trembled and stirred,
Though set so far
Its whirling frenzies
Appear like standing
In one self station.
It has not ranged,
And save for the wonder
Of once expanding
To be a nova,
It has not changed
To the eye of man
On planets over
Around and under
It in creation
Since man began
To drag down man
And nation nation.

TO EARTHWARD

Love at the lips was touch
As sweet as I could bear;
And once that seemed too much;
I lived on air

That crossed me from sweet things,
The flow of—was it musk
From hidden grapevine springs
Down hill at dusk?

I had the swirl and ache
From sprays of honeysuckle
That when they're gathered shake
Dew on the knuckle.

I craved strong sweets, but those
Seemed strong when I was young;
The petal of the rose
It was that stung.

Now no joy but lacks salt
That is not dashed with pain
And weariness and fault;
I crave the stain

Of tears, the aftermark
Of almost too much love,
The sweet of bitter bark
And burning clove.

When stiff and sore and scarred
I take away my hand
From leaning on it hard
In grass and sand,

The hurt is not enough:
I long for weight and strength
To feel the earth as rough
To all my length.

Three of Robert Frost's most quoted poems illustrate his ever-continuing growth and increasing variety. All three are from *A Witness Tree,* published in 1942, when the poet was sixty-seven. The first, "The Gift Outright," read as a Phi Beta Kappa poem at William and Mary College, is a poem that is both patriotic and thoughtful. The love of country is not expressed in screaming or hysterical flag-waving, but in a salvation of faith, in surrender to the land:

Such as she was, such as she would become.

The second, "A Considerable Speck," is witty and critical. Yet the wit is not bitter, and the criticism is only against those who are unthinking, too dull to act or even to reflect. The poet, he confesses with a twinkle, is relieved to find:

On any sheet the least display of mind.

"The Silken Tent" is a piece of sheer tenderness, a lyrical sonnet of gossamer beauty. As Mary Colum wrote in a review of *A Witness Tree:* "Here is the lyric in all its intensity, indeed, with a greater intensity than the lyrics the poet wrote when he was young. . . . These [later] lyrics have that wisdom, that power of revelation, which is time's last gift to the mature and powerful mind."

It is not so much the power of thought as the expressiveness that affects the reader. The spell of the lyrics is in their suggestion, in their half-revealed, half-concealed essence. What counts here is not so much the meaning as the shades of meaning.

THE GIFT OUTRIGHT

The land was ours before we were the land's.
She was our land more than a hundred years
Before we were her people. She was ours
In Massachusetts, in Virginia;
But we were England's, still colonials,
Possessing what we still were unpossessed by,
Possessed by what we now no more possessed.
Something we were withholding made us weak
Until we found out that it was ourselves
We were withholding from our land of living,
And forthwith found salvation in surrender.
Such as we were we gave ourselves outright
(The deed of gift was many deeds of war)
To the land vaguely realizing westward,
But still unstoried, artless, unenhanced,
Such as she was, such as she would become.

A CONSIDERABLE SPECK

A speck that would have been beneath my sight
On any but a paper sheet so white
Set off across what I had written there.
And I had idly poised my pen in air

To stop it with a period of ink
When something strange about it made me think.
This was no dust speck by my breathing blown,
But unmistakably a living mite
With inclinations it could call its own.
It paused as with suspicion of my pen,
And then came racing wildly on again
To where my manuscript was not yet dry;
Then paused again and either drank or smelt—
With loathing, for again it turned to fly.
Plainly with an intelligence I dealt.
It seemed too tiny to have room for feet,
Yet must have had a set of them complete
To express how much it didn't want to die.
It ran with terror and with cunning crept.
It faltered; I could see it hesitate;
Then in the middle of the open sheet
Cower down in desperation to accept
Whatever I accorded it of fate.

I have none of the tenderer-than-thou
Collectivistic regimenting love
With which the modern world is being swept.
But this poor microscopic item now!
Since it was nothing I knew evil of
I let it lie there till I hope it slept.

I have a mind myself and recognize
Mind when I meet with it in any guise.
No one can know how glad I am to find
On any sheet the least display of mind.

THE SILKEN TENT

She is as in a field a silken tent
At midday when a sunny summer breeze
Has dried the dew and all its ropes relent,
So that in guys it gently sways at ease,
And its supporting central cedar pole,
That is its pinnacle to heavenward
And signifies the sureness of the soul,
Seems to owe naught to any single cord,
But strictly held by none, is loosely bound
By countless silken ties of love and thought
To everything on earth the compass round,
And only by one's going slightly taut
In the capriciousness of summer air
Is of the slightest bondage made aware.

· · ·

Robert Frost began with lyrics and, after many successes
in blank verse monologues and "talking" narratives, he re-
turned to the singing line. When his work is viewed as a
whole, it will be seen that he never left the lyric for long.
The impulse grows with the convictions, and the convic-
tions grow with the years. The later songs reinforce the early
ones; they are perhaps somewhat riper, more mellow, "more
sure of all I thought was true."

"Good-Bye and Keep Cold," "A Prayer in Spring," and
the exquisite "Come In" were written during three widely
separated periods of the poet's life. But no analysis of change
or "evolution" or "development" can define their constant
appeal. Such poetry is ageless. It entices the reader with its
amiable surface of fact, and rewards him with its depth of
feeling. Never has poetry been more completely an act of
sharing, so friendly and so profound.

GOOD-BYE AND KEEP COLD

This saying good-bye on the edge of the dark
And the cold to an orchard so young in the bark
Reminds me of all that can happen to harm
An orchard away at the end of the farm
All winter, cut off by a hill from the house.
I don't want it girdled by rabbit and mouse,
I don't want it dreamily nibbled for browse
By deer, and I don't want it budded by grouse.
(If certain it wouldn't be idle to call
I'd summon grouse, rabbit, and deer to the wall
And warn them away with a stick for a gun.)
I don't want it stirred by the heat of the sun.
(We made it secure against being, I hope,
By setting it out on a northerly slope.)
No orchard's the worse for the wintriest storm;
But one thing about it, it mustn't get warm.
"How often already you've had to be told,
Keep cold, young orchard. Good-bye and keep cold.
Dread fifty above more than fifty below."
I have to be gone for a season or so.
My business awhile is with different trees,
Less carefully nurtured, less fruitful than these,
And such as is done to their wood with an axe—
Maples and birches and tamaracks.
I wish I could promise to lie in the night
And think of an orchard's arboreal plight
When slowly (and nobody comes with a light)
Its heart sinks lower under the sod.
But something has to be left to God.

A PRAYER IN SPRING

Oh, give us pleasure in the flowers to-day;
And give us not to think so far away
As the uncertain harvest; keep us here
All simply in the springing of the year.

Oh, give us pleasure in the orchard white,
Like nothing else by day, like ghosts by night;
And make us happy in the happy bees,
The swarm dilating round the perfect trees.

And make us happy in the darting bird
That suddenly above the bees is heard,
The meteor that thrusts in with needle bill,
And off a blossom in mid air stands still.

For this is love and nothing else is love,
The which it is reserved for God above
To sanctify to what far ends He will,
But which it only needs that we fulfil.

INTO MY OWN

One of my wishes is that those dark trees,
So old and firm they scarcely show the breeze,
Were not, as 'twere, the merest mask of gloom,
But stretched away unto the edge of doom.

I should not be withheld but that some day
Into their vastness I should steal away,
Fearless of ever finding open land,
Or highway where the slow wheel pours the sand.

I do not see why I should e'er turn back,
Or those should not set forth upon my track
To overtake me, who should miss me here
And long to know if still I held them dear.

They would not find me changed from him they knew—
Only more sure of all I thought was true.

COME IN

As I came to the edge of the woods,
Thrush music—hark!
Now if it was dusk outside,
Inside it was dark.

Too dark in the woods for a bird
By sleight of wing
To better its perch for the night,
Though it still could sing.

The last of the light of the sun
That had died in the west
Still lived for one song more
In a thrush's breast.

Far in the pillared dark
Thrush music went—
Almost like a call to come in
To the dark and lament.

But no, I was out for stars:
I would not come in.
I meant not even if asked,
And I hadn't been.

O Star (the fairest one in sight),
We grant your loftiness the right
To some obscurity of cloud—
It will not do to say of night,
Since dark is what brings out your light.
Some mystery becomes the proud.
But to be wholly taciturn
In your reserve is not allowed.
Say something to us we can learn
By heart and when alone repeat.
Say something! And it says "I burn."
But say with what degree of heat.
Talk Fahrenheit, talk Centigrade.
Use language we can comprehend.
Tell us what elements you blend.
It gives us strangely little aid,
But does tell something in the end.
And steadfast as Keats' Eremite,
Not even stooping from its sphere,
It asks a little of us here.
It asks of us a certain height,
So when at times the mob is swayed
To carry praise or blame too far,
We may choose something like a star
To stay our minds on and be staid.

Various critics have written of Frost as though he were two separate and almost opposed creators; they have contrasted the playful and lightly public bard with the painful and privately "dark" poet. The two cannot be separated. There is an unplumbed depth and an intensity of feeling in all but his most offhand verses, and if many of the lyrics as well as the monologues suggest an interior darkness, they have the color and quality of his New England woods, being lovely as well as dark and deep.

"A Servant to Servants" is filled with horror, but the grief and grimness are attended by understanding and a philosophic acceptance that "the best way out is always through." "Directive," a more cryptic poem, explores hidden meanings and scraps of old myths in its mixture of sadness and nostalgia. "Acquainted with the Night" and "Once by the Pacific" are records of a more personal melancholy touched with terror.

A SERVANT TO SERVANTS

I didn't make you know how glad I was
To have you come and camp here on our land.
I promised myself to get down some day
And see the way you lived, but I don't know!
With a houseful of hungry men to feed
I guess you'd find. . . . It seems to me
I can't express my feelings any more
Than I can raise my voice or want to lift
My hand (oh, I can lift it when I have to).
Did ever you feel so? I hope you never.

It's got so I don't even know for sure
Whether I *am* glad, sorry, or anything.
There's nothing but a voice-like left inside
That seems to tell me how I ought to feel,
And would feel if I wasn't all gone wrong.
You take the lake. I look and look at it.
I see it's a fair, pretty sheet of water.
I stand and make myself repeat out loud
The advantages it has, so long and narrow,
Like a deep piece of some old running river
Cut short off at both ends. It lies five miles
Straight away through the mountain notch
From the sink meadow where I wash the plates,
And all our storms come up toward the house,
Drawing the slow waves whiter and whiter and whiter.
It took my mind off doughnuts and soda biscuit
To step outdoors and take the water dazzle
A sunny morning, or take the rising wind
About my face and body and through my wrapper,
When a storm threatened from the Dragon's Den,
And a cold chill shivered across the lake.
I see it's a fair, pretty sheet of water,
Our Willoughby! How did you hear of it?
I expect, though, everyone's heard of it.
In a book about ferns? Listen to that!
You let things more like feathers regulate
Your going and coming. And you like it here?
I can see how you might. But I don't know!
It would be different if more people came,
For then there would be business. As it is,
The cottages Len built, sometimes we rent them,
Sometimes we don't. We've a good piece of shore

265

That ought to be worth something, and may yet.
But I don't count on it as much as Len.
He looks on the bright side of everything,
Including me. He thinks I'll be all right
With doctoring. But it's not medicine—
Lowe is the only doctor's dared to say so—
It's rest I want—there, I have said it out—
From cooking meals for hungry hired men
And washing dishes after them—from doing
Things over and over that just won't stay done.
By good rights I ought not to have so much
Put on me, but there seems no other way.
Len says one steady pull more ought to do it.
He says the best way out is always through.
And I agree to that, or in so far
As that I can see no way out but through—
Leastways for me—and then they'll be convinced.
It's not that Len don't want the best for me.
It was his plan our moving over in
Beside the lake from where that day I showed you
We used to live—ten miles from anywhere.
We didn't change without some sacrifice,
But Len went at it to make up the loss.
His work's a man's, of course, from sun to sun,
But he works when he works as hard as I do—
Though there's small profit in comparisons.
(Women and men will make them all the same.)
But work ain't all. Len undertakes too much.
He's into everything in town. This year
It's highways, and he's got too many men
Around him to look after that make waste.
They take advantage of him shamefully,
And proud, too, of themselves for doing so.

We have four here to board, great good-for-nothings,
Sprawling about the kitchen with their talk
While I fry their bacon. Much they care!
No more put out in what they do or say
Than if I wasn't in the room at all.
Coming and going all the time, they are:
I don't learn what their names are, let alone
Their characters, or whether they are safe
To have inside the house with doors unlocked.
I'm not afraid of them, though, if they're not
Afraid of me. There's two can play at that.
I have my fancies: it runs in the family.
My father's brother wasn't right. They kept him
Locked up for years back there at the old farm.
I've been away once—yes, I've been away.
The State Asylum. I was prejudiced;
I wouldn't have sent anyone of mine there;
You know the old idea—the only asylum
Was the poorhouse, and those who could afford,
Rather than send their folks to such a place,
Kept them at home; and it does seem more human.
But it's not so: the place is the asylum.
There they have every means proper to do with,
And you aren't darkening other people's lives—
Worse than no good to them, and they no good
To you in your condition; you can't know
Affection or the want of it in that state.
I've heard too much of the old-fashioned way.
My father's brother, he went mad quite young.
Some thought he had been bitten by a dog,
Because his violence took on the form
Of carrying his pillow in his teeth;

267

But it's more likely he was crossed in love,
Or so the story goes. It was some girl.
Anyway all he talked about was love.
They soon saw he would do someone a mischief
If he wa'n't kept strict watch of, and it ended
In father's building him a sort of cage,
Or room within a room, of hickory poles,
Like stanchions in the barn, from floor to ceiling.—
A narrow passage all the way around.
Anything they put in for furniture
He'd tear to pieces, even a bed to lie on.
So they made the place comfortable with straw,
Like a beast's stall, to ease their consciences.
Of course they had to feed him without dishes.
They tried to keep him clothed, but he paraded
With his clothes on his arm—all of his clothes.
Cruel—it sounds. I s'pose they did the best
They knew. And just when he was at the height,
Father and mother married, and mother came,
A bride, to help take care of such a creature,
And accommodate her young life to his.
That was what marrying father meant to her.
She had to lie and hear love things made dreadful
By his shouts in the night. He'd shout and shout
Until the strength was shouted out of him,
And his voice died down slowly from exhaustion.
He'd pull his bars apart like bow and bowstring,
And let them go and make them twang until
His hands had worn them smooth as any oxbow.
And then he'd crow as if he thought that child's play
The only fun he had. I've heard them say, though,
They found a way to put a stop to it.

He was before my time—I never saw him;
But the pen stayed exactly as it was
There in the upper chamber in the ell,
A sort of catch-all full of attic clutter.
I often think of the smooth hickory bars.
It got so I would say—you know, half fooling—
'It's time I took my turn upstairs in jail'—
Just as you will till it becomes a habit.
No wonder I was glad to get away.
Mind you, I waited till Len said the word.
I didn't want the blame if things went wrong.
I was glad though, no end, when we moved out,
And I looked to be happy, and I was,
As I said, for a while—but I don't know!
Somehow the change wore out like a prescription.
And there's more to it than just window-views
And living by a lake. I'm past such help—
Unless Len took the notion, which he won't,
And I won't ask him—it's not sure enough.
I s'pose I've got to go the road I'm going:
Other folks have to, and why shouldn't I?
I almost think if I could do like you,
Drop everything and live out on the ground—
But it might be, come night, I shouldn't like it,
Or a long rain. I should soon get enough,
And be glad of a good roof overhead.
I've lain awake thinking of you, I'll warrant,
More than you have yourself, some of these nights.
The wonder was the tents weren't snatched away
From over you as you lay in your beds.
I haven't courage for a risk like that.
Bless you, of course, you're keeping me from work,

But the thing of it is, I need to *be* kept.
There's work enough to do—there's always that;
But behind's behind. The worst that you can do
Is set me back a little more behind.
I sha'n't catch up in this world, anyway.
I'd *rather* you'd not go unless you must.

DIRECTIVE

Back out of all this now too much for us,
Back in a time made simple by the loss
Of detail, burned, dissolved, and broken off
Like graveyard marble sculpture in the weather,
There is a house that is no more a house
Upon a farm that is no more a farm
And in a town that is no more a town.
The road there, if you'll let a guide direct you
Who only has at heart your getting lost,
May seem as if it should have been a quarry—
Great monolithic knees the former town
Long since gave up pretense of keeping covered.
And there's a story in a book about it:
Besides the wear of iron wagon wheels
The ledges show lines ruled southeast northwest,
The chisel work of an enormous Glacier
That braced his feet against the Arctic Pole.
You must not mind a certain coolness from him
Still said to haunt this side of Panther Mountain.
Nor need you mind the serial ordeal
Of being watched from forty cellar holes

As if by eye pairs out of forty firkins.
As for the woods' excitement over you
That sends light rustle rushes to their leaves,
Charge that to upstart inexperience.
Where were they all not twenty years ago?
They think too much of having shaded out
A few old pecker-fretted apple trees.
Make yourself up a cheering song of how
Someone's road home from work this once was,
Who may be just ahead of you on foot
Or creaking with a buggy load of grain.
The height of the adventure is the height
Of country where two village cultures faded
Into each other. Both of them are lost.
And if you're lost enough to find yourself
By now, pull in your ladder road behind you
And put a sign up CLOSED to all but me.
Then make yourself at home. The only field
Now left's no bigger than a harness gall.
First there's the children's house of make believe,
Some shattered dishes underneath a pine,
The playthings in the playhouse of the children.
Weep for what little things could make them glad.
Then for the house that is no more a house,
But only a belilaced cellar hole,
Now slowly closing like a dent in dough.
This was no playhouse but a house in earnest.
Your destination and your destiny's
A brook that was the water of the house,
Cold as a spring as yet so near its source,
Too lofty and original to rage.
(We know the valley streams that when aroused

Will leave their tatters hung on barb and thorn.)
I have kept hidden in the instep arch
Of an old cedar at the waterside
A broken drinking goblet like the Grail
Under a spell so the wrong ones can't find it,
So can't get saved, as Saint Mark says they mustn't.
(I stole the goblet from the children's playhouse.)
Here are your waters and your watering place.
Drink and be whole again beyond confusion.

ACQUAINTED WITH THE NIGHT

I have been one acquainted with the night.
I have walked out in rain—and back in rain.
I have outwalked the furthest city light.

I have looked down the saddest city lane.
I have passed by the watchman on his beat
And dropped my eyes, unwilling to explain.

I have stood still and stopped the sound of feet
When far away an interrupted cry
Came over houses from another street,

But not to call me back or say good-bye;
And further still at an unearthly height,
One luminary clock against the sky

Proclaimed the time was neither wrong nor right.
I have been one acquainted with the night.

ONCE BY THE PACIFIC

The shattered water made a misty din.
Great waves looked over others coming in,
And thought of doing something to the shore
That water never did to land before.
The clouds were low and hairy in the skies,
Like locks blown forward in the gleam of eyes.
You could not tell, and yet it looked as if
The shore was lucky in being backed by cliff,
The cliff in being backed by continent;
It looked as if a night of dark intent
Was coming, and not only a night, an age.
Someone had better be prepared for rage.
There would be more than ocean-water broken
Before God's last *Put out the Light* was spoken.

Oh stormy, stormy world,
The days you were not swirled
Around with mist and cloud,
Or wrapped as in a shroud,
And the sun's brilliant ball
Was not in part or all
Obscured from mortal view,
Were days so very few
I can but wonder whence
I get the lasting sense
Of so much warmth and light.
If my mistrust is right
It may be altogether
From one day's perfect weather
When starting clear at dawn
The day went clearly on
To finish clear at eve.
I verily believe
My fair impression may
Be all from that one day
No shadow crossed but ours,
As through the blazing flowers
We went from house to wood
For change of solitude.

arch 26, 1962, was Robert Frost's eighty-eighth birth-
y. It was marked by three major events. Frost received the
arely awarded Congressional Medal from President Ken-
nedy at a White House ceremony. He was guest of honor
at a dinner attended by some two hundred notables at the
Pan American Union in Washington. His new volume, *In
the Clearing*, his first collection of new poems in fifteen
years, was published. The medal, the dinner, and the salvos
that greeted the book made Frost his country's accepted if
unofficial laureate.

All this was a confirmation of Frost's stature as a poet and
his status as a public figure. His eminence had been estab-
lished in January, 1961, when he recited "The Gift Out-
right" (see page 255) at the inauguration of President
Kennedy. It was the first time in the history of the United
States that a poet had been so honored. Frost had written
another poem for the occasion which he had intended to
read as a sort of "preface," but the sun was in his eyes, a
cold wind almost tore the paper from his hands, and, after
a few lines, he abandoned the attempt and recited "The Gift
Outright." The following is what was composed as a Gift
Outright of "The Gift Outright."

FOR JOHN F. KENNEDY
HIS INAUGURATION

With Some Preliminary History in Rhyme

Summoning artists to participate
In the august occasions of the state
Seems something artists ought to celebrate.
Today is for my cause a day of days.
And his be poetry's old-fashioned praise
Who was the first to think of such a thing.
This verse that in acknowledgement I bring
Goes back to the beginning of the end
Of what had been for centuries the trend;
A turning point in modern history.
Colonial had been the thing to be
As long as the great issue was to see
What country'd be the one to dominate
By character, by tongue, by native trait,
The new world Christopher Columbus found.
The French, the Spanish, and the Dutch were downed
And counted out. Heroic deeds were done.
Elizabeth the First and England won.
Now came on a new order of the ages
That in the Latin of our founding sages
(Is it not written on the dollar bill
We carry in our purse and pocket still?)
God nodded His approval of as good.
So much those heroes knew and understood,
I mean the great four, Washington,
John Adams, Jefferson, and Madison,—
So much they knew as consecrated seers

ney must have seen ahead what now appears,
They would bring empires down about our ears
And by the example of our Declaration
Make everybody want to be a nation.
And this is no aristocratic joke
At the expense of negligible folk.
We see how seriously the races swarm
In their attempts at sovereignty and form.
They are our wards we think to some extent
For the time being and with their consent,
To teach them how Democracy is meant.
"New Order of the ages" did we say?
If it looks none too orderly today,
'Tis a confusion it was ours to start
So in it have to take courageous part.
No one of honest feeling would approve
A ruler who pretended not to love
A turbulence he had the better of.
Everyone knows the glory of the twain
Who gave America the aeroplane
To ride the whirlwind and the hurricane.
Some poor fool has been saying in his heart
Glory is out of date in life and art.
Our venture in revolution and outlawry
Has justified itself in freedom's story
Right down to now in glory upon glory.
Come fresh from an election like the last,
The greatest vote a people ever cast,
So close yet sure to be abided by,
It is no miracle our mood is high.
Courage is in the air in bracing whiffs
Better than all the stalemate an's and ifs.

There was the book of profile tales declaring
For the emboldened politicians daring
To break with followers when in the wrong,
A healthy independence of the throng,
A democratic form of right divine
To rule first answerable to high design.
There is a call to life a little sterner,
And braver for the earner, learner, yearner.
Less criticism of the field and court
And more preoccupation with the sport.
It makes the prophet in us all presage
The glory of a next Augustan age
Of a power leading from its strength and pride,
Of young ambition eager to be tried,
Firm in our free beliefs without dismay,
In any game the nations want to play.
A golden age of poetry and power
Of which this noonday's the beginning hour.

"Away!" is Frost in his most whimsical mood. Although written in his eighties, it is as neatly made and as nimbly fanciful as any of his earlier and most accomplished rhymes. As if in answer to those who may be confused by his paradox of persiflage and profundity, Frost placed a teasing couplet near the end of *In the Clearing*:

It takes all kinds of in and outdoor schooling
To get adapted to my kind of fooling.

AWAY!

Now I out walking
The world desert,
And my shoe and my stocking
Do me no hurt.

I leave behind
Good friends in town,
Let them get well-wined
And go lie down.

Don't think I leave
For the outer dark
Like Adam and Eve
Put out of the Park.

Forget the myth.
There is no one I
Am put out with
Or put out by.

Unless I'm wrong
I but obey
The urge of a song:
I'm—bound—away!

And I may return
If dissatisfied
With what I learn
From having died.